CRACKED GLASSES

To contact Heather to speak at your church or school, send an e-mail to:
AuthorHeatherMarie@aol.com

Also by Heather Thompson Day:
Hook, Line, and Sinker

To order, **call 1-800-765-6955.**
Visit us at **www.reviewandherald.com** for information on other
Review and Herald® products.

CRACKED GLASSES

HEATHER THOMPSON DAY

MY POWER IS MADE
PERFECT IN WEAKNESS
2 Corinthians 12:9, NIV

R

REVIEW AND HERALD® PUBLISHING ASSOCIATION

Since 1861 | www.reviewandherald.com

Published by Review and Herald® Publishing Association, Hagerstown, MD 21741-1119.

Review and Herald® titles may be purchased in bulk for educational, business, fund-raising, or sales promotional use. For information, e-mail SpecialMarkets@reviewandherald.com.

The Review and Herald® Publishing Association publishes biblically based materials for spiritual, physical, and mental growth and Christian discipleship.

All Scripture references are from the *Holy Bible, New International Version.* Copyright © 1973, 1978, 1984, 2011 by Biblica, Inc. Used by permission. All rights reserved worldwide.

This book was
Edited by Megan Mason
Copyedited by Delma Miller
Cover design and photo by Daniel Anez / Review and Herald® Design Center
Interior designed by Emily Ford / Review and Herald® Design Center
Typeset: 11/13 minion pro

PRINTED IN U.S.A.

17 16 15 14 13   1 2 3 4 5

Library of Congress Cataloging-in-Publication Data
Day, Heather Thompson.
  Cracked glasses : my power is made perfect in weakness,
2 Corinthians 12:9 / Heather Thompson Day.
     p. cm.
1. Christian life—Seventh-Day Adventist authors. I. Title.
  BV4501.3.T4725 2013
  248.4'86732—dc23
                            2012032267
ISBN 978-0-8280-2564-5

Dedication

I am dedicating this book to my loving parents,
Joel and Vicki Thompson,
and grandparents,
Helen and Dick Stricklen,
whose love for me has seen no boundaries and no ending.
It is only by your faith in Christ and your effort to instill this same faith in me
that I have met the most beautiful Savior.
Surely it is your sweat, tears, and prayers that have made all the difference.

With all my love,
Heather

Contents

Dear Reader,

When I sat down to write this book, I thought for a moment about making it fictional, perhaps something *magical* in its telling—I could be anything I wanted to be in these pages, and you would never know. I could become beautiful and flawless, and you would have no choice but to believe that that is who I am. I could give myself a happy ending, make a vampire fall in love with me, slay dragons, or hunt demons—I could do those things.

I should warn you, however, before we go any further, that I am ordinary. There will be no pirates or wizards or secret worlds in my closet. My story is probably your story. *This is real life,* and I've learned that real life is often *better* than make-believe. Something beautiful happens when one person's story finds parallels in a stranger's. A bond germinates, a feeling of connectedness that whispers in our darkest moments, "You are not alone!" Both parties can part ways after this realization, *but neither will ever be the same* because something was born there, something incredible. So this is a *redemption* story. It is shattered dreams and lessons I've learned from losing; the most valuable lesson being that God's power is made perfect in our weakness, and that even though we may be a complete mess our Savior has no problems getting His hands dirty.

So let's take a 30-day journey together, you and I. Just know that at any moment something may be born here between the two of us, something that just may change us forever.

—Heather Thompson Day

Introduction

Christianity is a fight. It's a fight every day to hold yourself accountable and live life against the grain. I oftentimes think Christian writers lose themselves in this image we want to portray of perfection. God is perfect, but people are not, and it can be excruciating to constantly try to measure up to a force that's larger than life.

That is why I wrote this devotional. It is real-life stories geared toward young adults highlighting the truth, and the truth can be raw. This devotional is about figuring it all out. Balancing the struggle of trying to be "good," in a world where "good" is synonymous with boring, where exactly do Christians in a secular world fit in?

I once had a friend who told me that people are like glasses and sin is like rocks. Whether you are tossing pebbles at the glass and cracking it slightly, or smashing them with huge boulders that leave nothing but dust, damaged is damaged, and no one wants to drink out of a cracked glass. I've found out a secret, however, and in this devotional I try to share it. You see, I disagree with my friend. In my life I have learned that no matter how big the mistakes that ruptured me in two, or how damaging the blow was to my reputation or past, God doesn't just make new things; He makes things new.

I think God's cupboard would be filled to the brim with cracked glasses—cups with jagged lines and obvious glue marks from where He pressed the pieces back together. I think He not only drinks out of them, but has them lining His table so that anyone who happens to look can see His precious, cracked, beautifully handmade china. This book is about starting over. It's about patching the cracks and joining God's cupboard.

Chapter 1

Cracked Glasses

It is only imperfection that complains of what is imperfect. The more perfect we are, the more gentle and quiet we become towards the defects of others.
—*Joseph Addison*

A couple years ago I made my very first New Year's resolution. I decided it was time that I start trying to eat healthy. It was a necessary change in my life, considering up until then my body had been trained to be able to survive solely off of Cheetos and M&M's. It's almost a running joke in my family because I may go a whole day without eating, and then when I do, it's almost never something good for me. I'm not suggesting by any means that this is a good idea; I'm simply being honest.

It was on this path to healthful living that I became aware of a pretty intense discovery of myself. I was on my way to class one day that spring wearing my very athletic-looking Capri jogging sweats. My hair was in a tightly fitted ponytail and topped off with a black headband. I had a bottle of water in my purse and a half-eaten apple in my hand. I took my seat in class and noticed the kid next to me look me over. It hit me that I must appear very healthy to him. I looked pretty fit, I was wearing the right clothes, and in my hand was the proof: a half-eaten apple.

For a few seconds I reveled in this perception I thought he must have of me. For a moment, even if it was just to him, and even if it was just in my imagination, I felt like one of "those people." You know, "those people" who don't hit snooze on their alarm when it comes on, and instead jump out of bed, forgo their cars, and run to the gym. Those same people who order salads when going to restaurants, and the very same people whose faces turn into a look of disgust when they're behind me as I ask for extra mayo at Subway.

I looked healthy, so I felt healthy, and so for just a minute I was able to become whoever I wanted to be, and I chose to be one of "those people." I finished the remnants of my apple and then cracked open my bottle of cold water and felt like I was a walking advertisement for fitness as I put it to my lips. I half wanted to do some jumping jacks or bust into a sit-up as I toyed with this counterfeit vision of the new me.

As class ended I took my apple core and empty water bottle and headed out to my car. It was a gorgeous day outside, and I half jogged, half walked the distance to my Taurus. I had a kick in my step that wasn't usually present, because I was feeling good. I, after all, was healthy. When I got home, I did what I normally did at the time: I sat down next to my laptop, opened a package of Twinkies, and fiddled with some homework (and by homework I actually mean Facebook).

I didn't even realize it while I did it, but when I was finished, I noticed the empty water bottle beside my now empty Twinkie package and realized I wasn't healthy at all. I had made a big deal out of the apple, but the Twinkie didn't even faze me. That was second nature; consuming that came to me without thinking. I sat there stunned for a moment imagining my stomach mixing the contents together to form me: half healthy, half unhealthy, just depends on the day.

I thought about that moment a few days later when I finished having one of my morning devotionals and then jumped in the car and spat some heavy rap lyrics with Eminem. I had just filled my brain and heart with the Word of God, and then I mixed it with secularism. I mix God with the world and I form me: half spiritual, half unspiritual, just depends on the day.

Reflecting on this event in hindsight, I have noticed another parallel between my health life and my spiritual life. I almost never eat healthfully. I do, however, work out. It's not uncommon for you to find me on a summer day running a good five miles; I love running. My point is that I can be completely unhealthy on the inside, and yet on the outside appear as the picture of fitness. The scary thing about this is that sometimes what I do on the outside may taint the way I perceive myself on the inside. Because I know that my body can still run five miles a day, I then start to excuse all the unhealthy things I put into my body. Eventually I believe the façade that, regardless of what's going on inside me, as long as I "look healthy" I am healthy. This is all good and well until one day when my blood pressure rises because of my high level of cholesterol. I could be a walking heart attack and minimize my own issues because I have begun believing the image I am putting out. What we put out is important, but equally as important is what we put in. Likewise, if I am putting healthy stuff in but I am not doing the work, giving my body a chance to put healthy stuff out, then I am still unhealthy.

I invite you to join me for the next 30 days as we focus on getting healthy spiritually. Couple this devotional with at least a chapter of Bible reading a day, and let's work on putting the right foods in to fill that spiritual hunger. I really don't just recommend you pair your devotional reading with a scriptural reading; if I could shake you by the shoulders and firmly insist on it, I would. I refuse to make any baseless assumptions that by your just reading this devotional each day you will finish with a more favorable spiritual life.

I'm just a person. I'm working on being intensely mindful of every facet of my spiritual diet, but I don't have all the answers and there is nothing that I can say that will be a quick fix to whatever issues you have entering this 30-day journey with me. The Bible has to be the quencher of your thirst. In that Book is everything you will ever need in order to achieve salvation. I will tell you right now that if during these 30 days you ever miscalculate your time and have only a few minutes available to spend reading, put down this book and pick up His. That Book will save your life. I refuse to make you empty promises, but that is one you can be sure of. Reading the Bible daily for yourself, will change your life. Count on it. My intention with this book is simply that it will provide you with a sense of companionship in your journey through that Book. That said, you are on the right track here. You are working on putting healthy stuff into your body to soothe and cultivate the soul. But please, remember to also put stuff out. Exercise your mind through the power of Christian community. The biggest lesson I've learned so far in my life is that the only thing better than experiencing Christ individually is experiencing Him through community. Likewise, the only thing better than experiencing Christ through community, is experiencing Him individually. Those two concepts must be connected.

I made a different resolution this year than my previous year of attempting a healthful diet. I resolved that I would try to actually become a Christian, someone who follows Christ not just in word, but also in action. The kind of person that surrenders to His will not just in church school when I'm surrounded by my church friends, but also when I'm alone, accountable to no one but me.

I've made some pretty hefty mistakes in my life. If you checked my pockets right now, you may even find an empty Twinkie wrapper. The good news is that I don't have to be perfect, or even healthy, for God to notice me. One thing I can't stand is overhearing people talking about the mistakes of other people and hinting through their innuendos that certain people are too much baggage for Christ to carry. I know for a fact that God always finds a way to use us just as we are and change us, as long as our hearts are willing. Jesus Christ is all about saving sinners, so never worry that you are too much for His cross and never assume that someone else is either. Leave the mercy to the King of it. You just worry about meeting Him so you can accept it, and the directions you are providing other people.

I once watched a YouTube video in which a young guy was talking about this sex education video he had recently seen. It had a guy about to drink a bottle of water, and then out of nowhere like 50 people jump out of this van parked next to him and grab the water bottle from his hands, pass it around taking sips, licking the rim, and taking turns putting their dirty hands all over the plastic. They then hand the water bottle back to the guy, and a caption appears that reads "Who would want to drink from that bottle now?" Their point was that if you have too many sexual partners no one is ever going to want you.

After explaining what happened in the video, the young guy talking kind of shook his head in disbelief. "You want to know who wants that water bottle?" he said with a hint of a smile. "God does."

I couldn't agree with him more. God does. In spite of what you've done, God still wants you. Often when analyzing whether or not we are "good enough," we tend to look at ourselves through the perspective that our neighbors may see us. The thing that you have to remember is that God can see us through only one perspective and one relationship: the parent-child. In a normal, functioning parent-child relationship, there is nothing that child can do to escape their parents' love.

In the interpersonal communications course that I teach at a community college, we cover the six styles of love in relationships: ludic, which is characterized by fun and excitement; eros, which is characterized by beauty and sexuality; manic, which is characterized by extreme highs and extreme lows; storge, which is known as the friendship love because it is gradual and slow; pragma, which is loving someone more out of practicality than love; and last, agape, which is compassionate and selfless.

The textbook that I use in class says that many people wonder whether agapic love is actually attainable or more philosophical. Every time I get to agape, I tell my students that the closest they will ever get to achieving true, unconditional agapic love is in the parent-child relationship. Only in that relationship is love unconditional. In every other relationship—friendship, sibling, even lovers—if one party does something too destructive to the other, the relationship is severed. I'd venture to guess that in prison cells holding the most horrific serial killers, even that man or woman gets at least one or two visitors, and it isn't going to be their childhood next-door neighbors. It's mom and dad, because they don't know how to turn their love off.

God refers to Himself as our Father, as our Parent, for a reason. There is nothing we can do to separate ourselves from His agapic love, except of course if we simply choose to ignore it.

As I mentioned earlier, I once had a friend who told me that people are like glasses and sin is like rocks. Whether you are tossing pebbles at the glass and cracking it slightly, or smashing it with huge boulders that leave nothing but dust, damaged is damaged, and no one wants to drink out of a cracked glass.

I disagree with him, however. No matter how big the mistake that ruptured you in two, or how damaging the blows were to your reputation or past, it's a new day and a new year filled with new chances.

I think God's cabinets would be filled to the brim with cracked glasses. After all, He is the potter and you are His masterpiece. I can just imagine His cupboards containing cups with jagged lines and obvious glue marks from where He pressed the pieces back together. I think He not only drinks out of them, but has them lining His table so that anyone who happens to look can see His precious, cracked, beautifully handmade china. Don't believe what your sister, your neighbor, your ex, or your church elder told you; God loves cracked glasses. He's pacing back and forth racked with anxiety hoping desperately that you will come home. Who would want a cracked glass? God would. In fact, He's already paid the ultimate price for it.

For God so loved the world that he gave his one and only Son,
that whoever believes in him shall not perish but have eternal life.
—John 3:16

Chapter 2

Birds of a Feather

Christianity, if false, is of no importance, and if true,
of infinite importance. The only thing it cannot be is
moderately important.
—*C. S. Lewis*

What does Christianity look like? A speaker named José Rojas asked me this question daily during a Week of Spiritual Emphasis that was held by my university.

Immediately in my head I thought, *Well, not me.* If there was ever a poster board for Christianity, I am well aware my face wouldn't be on it. Instinctively, I'm not that nice of a person. I know this, because niceness is something the Lord has been smoothing my rough edges with. I know I'm not naturally nice, because as a child I was a bully. If you don't believe me, ask anyone who attended elementary school with me; I was a real tyrant. By nice in this sense I mean overtly friendly. Some people are really good at smiling, waving, and stopping to chat with everyone they know, no matter how slightly. That's just not me. It's not like I don't like people or have a chip on my shoulder; it's more like I just don't even think about it. I live in my head. If someone goes out of their way to break through the loud noise going on in my head, I of course respond in kind. I have been asking the Lord to work with me on initiating, because I know He will.

Instinctively, I am a loner. I have really learned to appreciate people and their stories during my entrance into adulthood, but as a child I didn't need people. I was just fine alone in my room with nothing but my imagination. Don't get me wrong; I like to be social. I'm just saying I don't need people to have fun. I am much more inclined to follow the pursuit of quality rather than quantity in dealing with friendships. I have literally one or two best girlfriends and then my family. I used to drink and party, but those people weren't my friends. In fact, I dare to say they never really knew me. Anyone who knows me without knowing my greatest passion in life, which is pursuing anything that God has for me, doesn't know me at all. Now I spend most of my Saturday nights at my parents' house. My brother and sister come over with their families and I sit on the couch laughing hysterically at all their stories.

As a child I was kind of the same way. I would make one best girlfriend in the class and drown everyone else out. People don't like that. Girls especially feel that you think you're better than they are if you don't include them. I never really assumed I was better; I just didn't think anything of it at all; I was just doing me.

I also always had this instinctive way of knowing just what buttons to push to make someone snap. I could plan something diabolical, push you to the edge, and then make you seem like the crazy one when you fell off the border. José Rojas put it best when he said, "I am not a good man; I just hang out with a very good God."

I believed him when he said that, because I could identify. Without God in my life, I'm pretty sure I'd still be nothing more than a 10-year-old girl, going through life with concern for no one but myself. The funny thing is I've always known God. Well, at least I've always known *of* Him. There has never been a moment in my life when I denied Him or even thought we weren't close. My entire life, as far as my memory can take me back, I've considered God to be my best friend, and now I realize He was just an acquaintance.

I didn't really know Him. I couldn't have, because if I had He would have rubbed off on me. Because I've lived on both sides of the fence, I can say this: it's positively impossible to truly fall in love with God and go on not caring about people. Those two philosophies cannot live in one heart. They are juxtaposed; they are complete contrasts. It's like the moon shining through the daylight and the sun showing through nighttime blackness; they just don't correlate.

God is in the business of loving people. If you want to know what Christianity looks like, I don't think you can find it individually. True Christianity can only be found in community. This has been one of the hardest concepts for me to understand, and also one of the hardest habits for me to change. If I want to be like Christ, I have to focus not just on how Christ works in me, but also on how I can work in community. People matter.

I was only fooling myself. God was not my best friend, and not because He didn't want to be, but because I was too busy not caring about the very thing He cares most about: people. I didn't care about them, and then I'd claim His friendship, not noticing how off base I was. I knew Him through other people and got glimpses of Him that He would show me from time to time when I would clean up my act. I knew Him through real Christians, Christians who loved other people, which to me is the face of Christianity. I knew Him through Weeks of Spiritual Emphasis and my mom and dad. I saw Him once in eighth grade when I felt the school system mistreated me, and at that moment I wanted nothing more than to be placed tightly into the palm of His hand. Devastation has a great way of bringing things into focus. I was 13 when I really started to know God. I had met Him in a Christian school, but I got to know Him in public school.

I got to know Him there because I met people who didn't, and for possibly the first time I saw what life is like when it's lived empty. In that moment I saw time dance without direction. I even experienced for myself what it is like when you live life, God-given life, from party to party, and I felt drained and unfulfilled. I was lucky because I had met God earlier, so I knew what it was like to be balanced by His fingertips, and thus I knew I was coming up short.

I decided to come back to my roots for college and entered a Christian institution, though it was not the same religion as mine my freshman year. I did that because I wanted to hang out with God again. I decided to trade in my late party nights for early pew mornings, and found peace in that exchange. I met people who were on fire for Christ, and I wanted that spark to be ignited in me. I met God again there, and this time I wasn't claiming anything but my need for Him.

I started reading my Bible, and not just opening it and praying for God to show me whatever verse I needed that day, as I had always done in the past. I started reading it from the beginning and I saw God's character revealed to me. There is no other book that we would start reading from the middle, so why do we do that with the Bible? At any rate, I began trying to understand who He was by actually shaking hands with Him first, and I've been changed.

I don't mean to downplay this book, because I am grateful you bought it and I do believe we will both learn from this experience; but I cannot stress to you enough how much the Bible changed my life. Devotionals are great, but I worry that so many of us are busy reading plenty of books *about* the Bible without ever actually reading the Bible itself. The Bible was made to stand alone. Only that Book can give you the change you may be seeking.

I'm not sure how it really happened, but the summer I came back from my freshman year in college I really felt Christ pointing me to Scripture. I had decided that I wanted to write books, and I promised Him that I would use only the talents that I believe He gave me in order to bring Him glory. That was the deal. I told Him that I would put in the work, be honest about the shortcomings I had experienced, and write them down in an attempt to praise His character. In return I asked that He would bless me and my work. God has the best way of blessing us. He does it in such a way that even those around us can be blessed. I wanted that.

When I sat down to start writing, I felt God directing me to Scripture. I realized He was telling me that I wasn't qualified to write about Him if I hadn't first met Him in His own Book. In the summer of 2006 I fell in love with the Bible. It took me the whole year to read it cover to cover, but I can still remember spending countless hours that summer curled up with this giant Book. If you can't tell, I'm gushing about this experience because I can see how far I've come. Reading the Bible was the turning point in the cultivation of my existence. He spoke to me through those pages, and I've never been the same. I want that for you.

In these next 29 days, if you open your heart and also open His Word, I'm telling you, God will change you. It doesn't matter who you are or where you are or how you got here. All that matters is that you are here, right now, seeking His guidance, and He is incredibly excited. It may not be something drastic. You may not pack a lifelong revelation into one summer the way I did, and that is OK. Each journey is different, and I think perhaps the best, most authentic way to change is when it happens slowly. Perhaps all you really need is someone to tell you that you are special and have a purpose. Your worth is immeasurable in Christ. That realization alone may plant the strongest seed.

I once heard a story about a watchmaker. He was a man who collected tons of watches. He had big ones, small ones, sparkly ones, and rustic ones. I suppose that that fact in itself is not so odd or memorable. Different people collect different things. The strange part of this story, though, is that none of these watches worked. He didn't sell them, he didn't give them away, and he didn't use them for spare parts. He collected them all, broken watches, and gave each one undivided attention.

His granddaughter asked him once, in the bluntness that only children can provide elegantly, why in the world he had so many broken watches. "If they don't work, you need to throw them away," she told him.

He picked up a gold one with a long chain that had probably once been a very expensive pocket watch, and flipped open the cover. "What time does this one say?" he asked her.

She responded, "3:00."

"And this one?" he asked, grabbing another.

"Twelve o'clock," she said, still unsure of his point. "Grandpa, these watches are no longer ticking," she added, hoping this would further her position that they were garbage. "What are you keeping them for?"

Smiling, he patted down the hair on her head. "You see," he began, picking up the watch stuck on noon, "at exactly two times a day, every watch in this room is right on time, and even in their brokenness, they are perfect. At exactly 12:00 noon today and 12:00 p.m. tonight, this watch right here will not be even a minute late."

She put her fingers on the watch in his hand, and within seconds replaced her frown with a smile. "I get it," she whispered.

I can't lie to you and say that as we speak, God's sculpting me a crown bigger than everyone else's. In fact, I can be brutally honest and tell you that I'm still broken and still racked with a sinful nature. However, I'm doing that while loving people. I may be filthy, but I'm hanging out with a God that's clean, and every day, a little more, I notice my instincts are changing. I notice that all of a sudden I'm truly caring about people. I guess if you hang out with someone long enough, they rub off on you.

God is that watchmaker, and we are the broken watches. Where everyone else would see garbage, God sees perfection. Even if you are not ticking like you used to, even if you are a mess inside and feel completely alone, God sees good in you. Even a broken watch is perfectly on time at two points every single day. I guess my question for you on day two as you go on and figure out where you fit into this scheme of life is simply What time is it?

And so we know and rely on the love God has for us.
God is love. Whoever lives in love lives in God, and God in them.
—1 John 4:16

Chapter 3

Satan Told Me God Was Angry

Though we are incomplete, God loves us completely. Though we are
imperfect, He loves us perfectly. Though we may feel lost and without
compass, God's love encompasses us completely. . . . He loves every one of us,
even those who are flawed, rejected, awkward, sorrowful, or broken.
—*Dieter F. Uchtdorf*

Sometimes I feel as though God is far away from me, like He's turned His back to me because He's frustrated with the continual mistakes I make. We, as humans, can only tell someone not to do something so many times before their continuation to do the very thing we advised them against makes us angry. Sometimes I feel as if God is angry with me.

Sometimes I'll avoid prayer, hoping that what I have just done will blow over in His mind till He forgets. I'll still pray, just not really. I refrain from asking Him anything that would require me to dig deeper and ask something of myself. I put our relationship on standby for a few moments, because I can't bear to call His name knowing I've made a fool of Him before the heavenly hosts.

That's usually the thought that puts me into such deep sorrow that I can't sleep at night. Not always the fact that I sinned, but that I sinned on purpose. It wasn't an accident; it was a choice, a choice I made again. I have a hard time sleeping at night when I think of the way I betrayed Him. I quit trying to avoid sin because of fear a long time ago. I used to try hard to make perfect decisions because I was scared of His wrath otherwise. I realized, however, that God isn't supposed to be served out of fear but out of love, and that's how I now try to treat Him.

Now when I choose Satan's offerings over God's (and that is what I'm doing when I sin, choosing Satan), I feel racked with grief and not out of fear, but out of the sheer pain I know God must feel as I choose the enemy over the friend. Only in dealing with God and Satan would we ever do that. No one in their right mind would ever have any sort of dealings with the complete enemy of someone they loved in any other circumstance than spiritual matters. It just wouldn't happen. Loyalty is a value in American society. It's a statute that is sought. We can forgive a lot of other digressions in one another, as long as we feel loyalty.

As a child I used to wonder why God didn't just destroy Lucifer after he fell. I look around the world and I see so much devastation and heartache, and there have been moments that I questioned why Christ would even have created a being that He knew would end up being rebellious. God is powerful. He could have zapped Lucifer out of existence before he even had a chance to incite doubt into the minds of his peers.

Likewise, in the Garden of Eden, why even create a tree that you knew would tempt them? Why allow the serpent to be a part of that world? Why even give him a voice box to deceive? I remember reading in Ellen White's writings that Satan never believed that God would actually allow Adam to die. He thought that once Eve took a bite of the apple he had won, because he thought God would have to allow sin to occur in the same world as His holiness forever. By deceiving them, he was sure that sin would perpetually exist. You see, up until this point no one had ever died. Death had never existed until our world fell, and so Satan could not even conceive what death was.

"It was Satan's plan that Adam and Eve should by disobedience incur God's displeasure; and then, if they failed to obtain forgiveness, he hoped that they would eat of the tree of life, and thus perpetuate an existence of sin and misery. But after man's fall, holy angels were immediately commissioned to guard the tree of life. Around these angels flashed beams of light having the appearance of a glittering sword. None of the family of Adam were permitted to pass that barrier to partake of the life-giving fruit; hence there is not an immortal sinner" (*Patriarchs and Prophets*, p. 60).

She also said that God allowed Adam to be laid to rest out of mercy. That when he witnessed the death of the first flower, he mourned for that plant the way you and I would mourn for our family. He realized what he had done, and he couldn't stomach it. After nearly 1,000 years God allowed Adam to be put out of the constant misery of walking around each day on a planet that he had destroyed.

"Adam's life was one of sorrow, humility, and contrition. When he left Eden, the thought that he must die thrilled him with horror. He was first made acquainted with the reality of death in the human family when Cain, his first-born son, became the murderer of his brother. Filled with the keenest remorse for his own sin, and doubly bereaved in the death of Abel and the rejection of Cain, Adam was bowed down with anguish. He witnessed the wide-spreading corruption that was finally to cause the destruction of the world by a flood; and though the sentence of death pronounced upon him by His Maker had at first appeared terrible, yet after beholding for nearly a thousand years the results of sin, he felt that it was merciful in God to bring to an end a life of suffering and sorrow" (*ibid.*, p. 82).

It is only now that I really understand why God allowed all of these things to happen. Now I get why He permitted destruction, even if it meant the crucifixion of His own Son. It is because God wants to be served out of love, not fear. God is love. I think we say that sometimes but we don't really stop to think about what that means. The word "God" is synonymous with the word "love." God does not want or need your fear, just love.

God, then, must often be lonely. Thousands, millions even, claim to be His friend, yet neglect that one defining friendship virtue: love based on pure and utter loyalty to God. That should be your common denominator between purity and Christ. We should avoid sin on that basis alone. Not because we fear the consequences, not because we want to feel good about ourselves, not because we want to be respected as a spiritual beacon. I'd even go as far as to say not because we want to go to heaven. Sin should be avoided on the purely sincere basis of our complete submission to God through love and loyalty. We should turn our backs to Satan's temptations because the thought of coordinating any type of trade with the enemy of our Father is vile to us.

And so when I do mess up, when I do exhibit how weak my friendship is, when I'm a traitor to the best friend I've ever had, I sometimes feel as though He wants nothing to do with me, and that thought hurts. However, when I was reading one morning in *Steps to Christ*, a tiny, precious book written by Ellen G. White, I was comforted.

She writes, "The enemy of good blinded the minds of men, so that they looked upon God with fear; they thought of Him as severe and unforgiving. Satan led men to conceive of God as a being whose chief attribute is stern justice—one who is a severe judge, a harsh, exacting creditor" (pp. 10, 11).

As I read those words that morning, I was humbled. I realized that God, the same God that I had been avoiding since the evening before, and the same God that I had written off through my surface-level prayers, that God was speaking to me. He made an effort to seek me out, and in His ever-powerful mercy reminded me that His mission to earth was not to tally the errors of humanity, but to scribble in the sand in the name of mercy. I forgot that God was love, and that morning Ellen White reminded me that not only is God love, but that I need to reciprocate that love through loyalty.

Sometimes I write because I feel a need to express something. Sometimes it's only because it's my job, and other times it's because I need to put filler where there would otherwise be empty space. Sometimes, however, I write because it frees me. Because if I don't share what God has done for me, then I haven't really believed He's done anything. Today, I wrote because Ellen White reminded me that God is love, and so I thought that maybe I could remind you.

Yes, Satan told me God was angry, but Jesus showed me He was love. Actions speak louder than words, and the power of the cross is so thunderous it's deafening.

Let love and faithfulness never leave you;
bind them around your neck,
write them on the tablet of your heart.
—Proverbs 3:3

Chapter 4

Apple Valley Massacre

You have to forget your last marathon before you try another.
Your mind can't know what's coming.
—Frank Shorter

When I was about 10 years old, my mother entered me into a race for the entire town put on by our local grocery store, Apple Valley. I was in it to win it. I was determined and focused that this moment would be mine forever. The race was divided into heats by age and sex. I had about 15 to 20 other 10-year-old girls who could taste the victory in the race with me. I prayed many heartfelt and sincere prayers to the Big Guy for strength and dominance.

The girl next to me had two long pigtailed braids that I hoped would slow her down if the wind slapped them across her cheeks. On the other side was a chubbier girl whose eyes had already started to water at the mere anxiety of what was about to take place. I'd be sure to send her crying to her mother.

Three people down and to my right was my most worthy opponent. She looked sturdy and athletic and kept her hair in a tightly fitted bun. She spotted me at the starting line and narrowed her eyebrows in my direction. I smirked back at her because I wasn't scared. I knew what I had to do and had already run through the race in my mind, and each time I was the victor. The winner would receive some kind of gift certificate to Apple Valley, but my mother could have that; I was racing for dignity.

I had never been in a real race before, besides just horsing around for fun with my sister. The night before the race I could hardly sleep in anticipation of the big day. I am not sure what even made me enter the race to begin with. I was 10. I didn't know anything about track or racing. I wasn't all that athletic, either; I was extremely skinny, and I cried at the first sign of hard work or pain. For whatever reason, though, I had it in my mind that not only was I going to run this race—I was going to win it.

As we all stood lined up there I can remember the strongest sense of fight or flight taking over my little body. I am not exaggerating this either. It's been more than 10 years since that day, and yet if I close my eyes I can still feel the breeze in the air and see the starting line. This was the first thing I ever really wanted on my own. No one told me to do it, no one suggested I would be good at it, no one coaxed me into it. It was a decision I came to on my own, and for whatever reason I felt pride in that.

At the sound of the gun we took off, and I kicked my legs like a wild stallion. I pummeled the earth and took my breath in ferocious gulps of air that burned my lungs. I pumped my arms and lifted my knees, just as I had in my imagination. I ran as if someone had lit a fire beneath my feet. I poured my heart into that race, and I lost. I didn't even make second or third place. The chubby girl and pigtails both beat me. I would have come in dead last had I not tripped a girl with sandals two steps after the gun. I was probably the slowest girl at the park that day.

As I collapsed in the grass I felt the sun beat so heavy on my face I thought it would scorch my skin. I let the breeze kiss my cheeks and felt a single tear roll from the duct of my eye. Then, as if a dam had collapsed, a million tears flowed from my eyes, much like those of a child whose ice cream falls off the cone. The moment that was supposed to be mine forever was, but in defeat.

I don't know what in the world made me try out for the middle school track team several years after that, but I did. Perhaps somewhere in the recesses of my mind it was like a vendetta I had to solve against myself. I remember my first race. I wore these white knee-high socks and bright white eye shadow that I swear was in at the time. My friends were all there, and to lose would have been a huge embarrassment. I was one of the only girls completely unprepared and in sneakers; track runners wear spikes that allow their feet to be lighter and faster. I had big, chunky sneakers that my mom probably bought me from a store that was more about economic friendliness than style. Luckily for me, I won that race. I didn't lose a race again until some years later in high school. I can still remember the girl I lost to. She had long legs and blond hair, and was exceptionally tan. Losing for the second time hurt, but it didn't stop me from running the next one.

You see, that's life—wins and losses. Had I let that Apple Valley massacre keep me from ever running again, I wouldn't have all the memories I hold now. I wouldn't have gone to state in the 4x100-meter relay my freshman year of high school. I wouldn't have qualified again for state in the same race my junior year, and I certainly wouldn't have gotten a college track scholarship and made it to nationals. I wouldn't have this box of medals that I still keep under my bed, and I wouldn't have learned what it felt like to put your heart into something, and still come up empty.

Running track for those six or so years of my life taught me so many valuable lessons. I learned how to compete graciously, how to work hard at something without crying, how to fall in front of a stadium filled with people and still get back up and finish the race. I learned how to have confidence in my own abilities even when standing at a starting line against girls who looked physically superior. I learned patience. I learned how to put so much energy into something that I actually vomited when I was finished and collapsed in the grass alone and exhausted. I learned how to win, but most important, I learned how to lose. I'll never be an Olympian, but I can sleep at night knowing I didn't quit.

I think Satan knows how hard it is for us to lose. He banks on our misfortunes and hopes the tears in our eyes will sting hard enough to keep us down. He sets us up, hopes we make bad choices, and then, when and if we do, tells us we are unfit to run to the arms of God. No matter what happened to you this past year, last summer, or when you were 10 years old and in a foot race, don't let it keep you from getting back up and trying again. If there's breath in your lungs, you're still in the race. If there is blood in your veins, you're still in the race. If your heart is still beating, you're still in the race. You are still in this race, and that alone is reason enough to keep running.

Do you not know that in a race all the runners run,
but only one gets the prize?
Run in such a way as to get the prize.
—1 Corinthians 9:24

Chapter 5

Christianity on Autopilot

Being born in a Christian home does not make you a Christian.
—E. Stanley Jones

I heard myself say I was a Christian the other day, and I wondered if, had I not said that, people would have assumed it anyway.

I recently read a book that I had started reading earlier in my life but must have placed back on the shelf. The title is *Tuesdays With Morrie*, a true story written by Mitch Albom. I'm not planning on reciting the book for you; you can read it on your own time. But I do want to share with you how this book has changed me.

The premise of the book is simply the story of a once-college student, now successful sportswriter, who reconnects with his university mentor, Morrie, who is now dying from amyotrophic lateral sclerosis (ALS), better known as Lou Gehrig's disease, a brutal and unforgiving illness of the neurological system.

The book, though beautifully written, didn't hit me all at once or knock me off kilter at my initial digestion. Rather, it has had a much more subtle impact that has left me hungry for people. You see, we all want to influence this world. We each have our secret fantasies of causing change or doing something extraordinary worth long-lasting memory. We all want to invoke revolution through Christ, or do something that sets us apart. You know every human has this innate desire to do something memorable with their life because of how Western culture portrays obituaries. You will never read an obituary that says "She partied a lot" or "He had good hair." No, we try to put together a list of the accomplishments or achievements that this person's life provided. We try to recognize the good. We all want, or rather should want, to be the face of Christianity, and then we go out into the world and close our eyes to people. Not just people, either—His people.

I once read in a *Chicken Soup* book that a mother asked her 10-year-old son how he thought you could get people to heaven, and his answer still sits heavy on the palate of my tongue like a taste that, no matter how hard I try, I can't rinse out. "You love them there," he said.

It's hard to dislike someone who is portraying love to you. Gandhi used this philosophy in his attempts to liberate India. He portrayed a very inclusive view of religion. Though a Hindu, he often quoted from the Koran, Torah, and Bible. He believed that the power of love and peaceful demonstrations would be harder to ignore than combat and violence. He got this from Jesus Christ.

Jesus said in Matthew 5:39, "But I tell you, do not resist an evil person. If anyone slaps you on the right cheek, turn to them the other cheek also." Jesus was the utter picture of complete love and humility shown even to antagonists. Perhaps this is why Gandhi said, "I like your Christ, I do not like your Christians. Your Christians are so unlike your Christ."

And so here's my appeal, my altar call or point of passion. Are we, as Christians, mirroring the love of Christ? Do we love others to heaven? In *Tuesdays With Morrie* Morrie sits at the end of his life and is suddenly acutely aware of the desperate need people have for relationships. He drives home the fact that people are always looking to donate money to a good cause, but more often than not it's time that would be best given. Time—the easiest of things, it seems, but yet the hardest for us to give away.

So I have to ask: What are we, as Christians, really doing for others? What are we doing personally to make sure that all the neighboring towns are feeling our presence? Do all the neighboring nursing homes, all the single-parent children, and all the broken-down and wayward teenagers know we are here? Are we loving them somewhere? anywhere?

I think more often than not we pass the buck. We leave missions to the missionaries and do our Christian thing from the pew. We sing in song service and pray for the homeless and then pass by the people in our everyday lives that may need us. I personally think that one day I am going to be held accountable for every person I was "too busy" to reach out to. One day I am going to stand before God, and He's going to inform me of all the people He strategically placed into my life and then show me how I passed by them.

Ellen White says in *Prophets and Kings*, "As with Solomon, so with Rehoboam—the influence of wrong example led many astray. And as with them, so to a greater or less degree is it today with everyone who gives himself up to work evil—the influence of wrongdoing is not confined to the doer" (p. 94). This is a powerful statement. I think we often excuse our bad actions by saying we are not affecting anyone but ourselves, and yet, somehow, when we do something good we assume we are doing our part in assuring someone else's salvation. If the good things we do affect others, why wouldn't the bad?

White continues: "No man liveth unto himself. None perish alone in their iniquity. Every life is a light that brightens and cheers the pathway of others, or a dark and desolating influence that tends toward despair and ruin. We lead others either upward to happiness and immortal life, or downward to sorrow and eternal death. And if by our deeds we strengthen or force into activity the evil powers of those around us, we share their sin" (*ibid.*). No one lives alone. We are all connected, and the way you live is helping either to enforce the life of Christ and His work or to destroy it.

Sometimes I forget how lucky I am. I was born Christian. I came into this world on the brink of truth. My parents struggled and worked extra hours all in an effort to lace me with Christian education, and at some point I think I have to ask myself, What am I doing with it? I've got eight years of elementary school, a bachelor's and a master's degree from a private college where I've been pumped full with Christ, and what have I done personally to prove it? In all honesty, sometimes it feels like nothing.

To me, the most beautiful thing about evangelizing is that it doesn't take much to do it. Sometimes it takes nothing more than a conversation and the dedication of a little time to be a friend. And there may not be tons of people craving religion (not that they are aware of, anyway), but there are always people craving friendship, there are always people just looking for someone to talk to, someone to confide in, even more simply, just someone to listen.

I know I've said this before, but it's only because I believe it so passionately. I have met Christ through His Word, and I have figured out that the closest way to follow in His footsteps is by embracing His people. For some reason that's hard for us to do, and I of all people get that. I know as much as anyone that it's easy to get so consumed in everyday life that it's all we can do to just look out for ourselves. We don't have the time or energy to carry someone else's cross, but trust me, it is our Christian mission to dig deep. If you get nothing else from this devotional entry, please walk away with this thought: learn to treasure people, and you will learn to walk with Christ.

And so you'd think that as Christians, as Bible scholars and prayer warriors, as pastors' kids and faith leapers, as believers and seekers, as churchgoers and praise singers, as representations of Christ, we'd find that that would be involuntary. You'd think friendliness would be like blinking, something we do on autopilot. You'd think that we would, on reflex, share the love of God through companionship. You'd think that for us, that would be routine. You'd think that. But is it?

Above all, love each other deeply, because love
covers over a multitude of sins.
—1 Peter 4:8

Chapter 6

Using Your Umbrella

Preach the gospel at all times. When necessary, use words.
—Francis of Assisi

In college I learned one of the most important lessons of my life: People may not remember exactly what you did or what you said, but they will always remember how you made them feel.

I think far too often we suppose that we have to go to different countries as missionaries to play a part in showing Christ's behaviors. At least I know I am guilty of that. My Eurocentric nature gets the best of me, and I think that Christ's character is something needed for everyone else. That was until college, that is, when I was reminded in a small way that God is not only a God of big gestures and huge moves, but also a God of the small things: the tiniest of moments that impact with just enough power to leave imprints on the hearts of those touched.

My freshman year of college I had to get my immunizations. I had to get a meningitis shot and a tuberculosis test. Just to add some background information, I am terrified of shots. I was extremely grumpy and upset about the whole ordeal. I was 18 years old at the time and made my mother hold my hand through the entire thing.

I can remember as a child when my sister got her tetanus shot. I prayed in my head and asked God for some other method to be developed, some oral pill that would work just as well, by the time I was old enough to need the shot. In eighth-grade biology class we had to figure out what blood type we were. It took me the whole class period to be convinced that it was only a prick and that my finger wouldn't fall off. I don't like pain, I cry when something hurts, and I am no hero. I can't tell you how mortified I was when I learned how babies come out.

My senior year of high school the coach of the women's basketball team asked me to try out because he needed some sprinters. He knew I was excellent at track and said basketball would be a breeze. The first day of tryouts a girl threw me a pass before I was ready, and the ball smacked me in my face. Without saying a word, I dropped my arms, walked off the court, grabbed my coat and keys, and left, never to return again. From then on my only experience with basketball was cheerleading at the games, and even then I made sure to always scan the court before tip-off to find a place to take shelter should any stray balls come flying in my direction. And don't even get me started on dodgeball in gym class. I'd skip and hide out in the locker room. I hate getting hurt.

It was scorching hot when we went into the doctor's office, but while inside we could hear the thunder rolling from beyond the building. As we went to leave, my mother and I stood paralyzed at the door, staring at this monsoon of wind and rain and trying to figure out how long we would have to stand there before we could run to the car. I was already bitter. I just wanted to go home, crawl on my couch, and lick my wounds from my terrible visit. I thought it would have been nice if someone had had the courtesy to offer me a wheelchair, but it didn't happen. I made a mental note to cancel any dental appointments I had in the next month, and contemplated purchasing a rubber ball that I could live in for the rest of my life.

We were discussing our options for traversing the rain when this young girl in her 20s came up and said, "Hey, I was listening to you guys, and I have an umbrella. If you want, I'll walk you to your car." So sure enough, she walked my mom to her door and then me to mine, and then was on her way.

I know that may seem so microscopic, so insignificant, in the large scheme of anything. However, in that moment I was touched. Her ambivalent gesture has had me reeling for years now. It impacted me on the importance of these modest actions and brought tangible meaning to the saying "a little can go a long way."

I was so touched that the girl wasn't so concerned with getting herself to her car that she brushed right past us and went on her own way. Instead, she seized the opportunity to do something nice for someone else. Imagine how amazing the world would be if we all started seizing all of the small moments and doing these little random acts of kindness. Pay for the guy behind you at the drive-through, wait a few extra seconds while holding a door open, hand spare change to the kid in line who doesn't have enough, smile at a stranger and mean it. Let's do our part to put goodness out in a world holding a lot of bad, even if all we can muster is the small random acts of kindness.

I think of that girl often now. She's the reason I pause to hold open doors for others, don't take the last dessert on the tray, and compliment someone if I think they look nice or notice they've had a haircut. So much of life is in the small stuff, the tiniest moments that you think would mean nothing and yet somehow when all added together seem to make the most significant differences. If you wait for the big moments to arise in order to do something for someone else, you may spend your entire life waiting.

A student gave a speech in one of my classes once about how beneficial smiling is. She followed the research of Ron Gutman and told the class that smiling actually stimulates our brain reward mechanisms in a way that even chocolate cannot compete with. Chocolate is a well-regarded pleasure inducer. British researchers found that just one smile can provide the same pleasure-inducing results in the brain as up to 2,000 bars of chocolate. The same study also suggested that smiling is just as stimulating on the brain as receiving $25,000 in cash. Statistically, many children may smile up to 400 times per day, and at $25,000 a smile, this means that there are millions of kids in this world who know what it feels like to be Bill Gates.

Have you ever noticed that when you see someone else yawn you find yourself yawning? We can infect people with our tiredness. Likewise, smiling and happiness is also contagious. It literally spreads from one person to another. Harvard researchers actually did a study on this and found that one person's happiness quite literally infects those around them. We have metaneurons in our brain that force us to mimic other people's facial expressions. So when we smile at someone, the metaneurons in their brain send messages to their smile muscles that replicate your smile. It's an automatic reflex in our brains. This allows you to stimulate someone else's brain by causing their pleasure inducers to be roused all because you flashed them one smile.

My life has been changed ever since I started challenging myself to pursue some of these everyday chances that we have to do something nice for someone else and show others, right where we are, what Christianity is all about. You never know what small act of kindness someone else may treasure forever. It is these acts that plant seeds. Someone else may do the watering, another the sowing and ground cultivation, but no matter how you slice it, the seed is still essential. Even if all that seed is is a simple smile or making sure you are not too busy to help a stranger get out of the rain.

For the mouth speaks what the heart is full of.
—Matthew 12:34

Chapter 7

Hold On, God—I Got a Text!

Gratitude bestows reverence,
allowing us to encounter everyday epiphanies,
those transcendent moments of awe
that change forever how we experience life and the world.
—*John Milton*

It's kind of like God invites you into His house for a much-needed heart-to-heart. Right after the songs of praise and a little bit of Bible study, He begins to open up and let you know what He really called you here to say. The only problem is right as He begins to speak you whip out your cell phone and start playing Tetris. Tetris, Pac-Man, Bejeweled—you even fire up an entire conversation via text. I'd imagine He'd eventually give up talking, though you may not ever notice.

This is not about judgment; it's simply a reminder on respect. I have to ask my technologically savvy generation of Christians to please set aside the simple hour and a half of church to get off your cell phone and let God speak. If we truly believe that our pastors are inspired by God to speak to us at church, you'd think we could give them the respect of vibrate. No one's even forcing you to turn the thing off; wouldn't want to neglect that ever-important "missed call."

My pastor gave a sermon once before Christmas break about how God is coming and he wonders if the church will be sleeping. I can't speak for the entire church, or even all the youth, but I will say that from where I sit, a lot of young people will not be sleeping, but they may be texting, Myspacing, and Facebooking themselves right into the Second Coming. We may miss the entire book of Revelation because we'd rather watch videos on YouTube.

The time you spend with God, of all the things you will do in this life, deserves your utmost respect. We are talking about Christ here. The same Jesus of Nazareth who allowed Himself to be brutally beaten. The same Savior dressed from robes of light in heaven that let His children hang

His body bare and naked on a cross. That same Lord who is now forever fully man and fully God is allowing us into His house, and, this is just my opinion, I'm going to guess He wants our undivided attention.

We read in Scripture that this peaceful Jesus got seriously upset when people desecrated His temple. When the Jews forgot that God's house was holy, Jesus got angry.

We can see the scene play out in Matthew 21:12-14: "Jesus entered the temple courts and drove out all who were buying and selling there. He overturned the tables of the money changers and the benches of those selling doves. 'It is written,' he said to them, '"My house will be called a house of prayer,"' but you are making it "a den of robbers."'"

That was Jesus. The same Jesus who in His own defense trial stood most of the hours silent. The same Jesus full of peace and love, who was slow to anger and quick to mercy, that same Jesus was seriously offended at the lack of respect shown in His father's house. Clearly this is an issue to take note of.

Jesus saw people disrespecting the home, the dwelling place, of the Trinity, and He was offended. You have to think back to when the Israelites carried the ark of the covenant around with them everywhere: it was regarded as holy, for they knew that the Lord dwelled there. The reverence and respect for the ark was extremely important to them. When David asked God if he could build a temple, God told him no. God told David no, the man whom we constantly see Christ referring back to throughout later passages with adoration and love. David was a man of war, and God didn't want a man of blood to build His temple. God respects His house, and somewhere through time I think we too have forgotten.

I would not be surprised if Jesus took a stroll through my church or your church, and also became angry. I mean c'mon, I've heard people complaining about hearing cell phones at the beach because they think it ruins the atmosphere. We comply when asked to turn our phones off in a movie theater for the respect of Hollywood. I can honestly say I see fewer people with phones out gaming during a movie than I do at church. You'd think no one would even have to ask for that same respect to be shown toward Christ, and yet here I am, asking.

We all make mistakes. I don't mean to point the finger so callously, because I am sure there are things I have been doing that I didn't put much thought into that someone else may one day come up to me about and open my eyes to my error. The case can be made for ignorance, but not persistently.

My request is simple, and I really wouldn't have brought it up if it wasn't becoming such a noticeable problem. I know this does not apply to everyone, but I think it should still be said. Let us make new covenants with ourselves, assuring that when we are in God's house on His day we'll put away our cell phones. It really is a slap in His face, and to be honest, there are enough people in this world willing to do that intentionally. Let us give the Being that allows breath to remain in our lungs the decency of a time-out for Him to speak, and for us to do nothing but listen. Trust me, your phone will be there tomorrow, but your soul may not be.

Therefore, since we are receiving a kingdom that cannot be shaken,
let us be thankful, and so worship God acceptably with reverence and awe.
—Hebrews 12:28

Chapter 8

Painting People

We become not a melting pot but a beautiful mosaic.
Different people, different beliefs,
different yearnings, different hopes, different dreams.
—*Jimmy Carter*

(I have written the following story in honor of my sister
Natasha Thompson.)

I am biracial. My mother is White, and my father is Black. Living within the confined walls of my colorful family, I was always safe. When I was 4, however, my "racial safety helmet" was about to be unfastened. It was then that I was able to begin preschool. I was actually excited to start preschool, because my sister was already in the very prestigious second grade, and she was my idol. I would have sold my soul to wrap my fingers around her purple *Beauty and the Beast* lunch box.

The night before, I remember tossing in my bed, unable to stifle my tiny body into the yellow covers, which seemed to cling to my perspiring skin. When I picture it now, I'm wearing my pink silk pajamas. I wore them every night because my mother wore silk pajamas, and I would have given anything to resemble my mommy, who to me was my twin. Whether I really wore those pajamas has escaped me now. Time often finds its way into your head. It smoothes out the edges of your crinkled past and creates this faulty reality of how you interpreted the event.

The day preschool started I willingly adventured off to the daunting of a new era. I could have sworn I was a woman as my father walked me down the hallway and through those glass doors, which would in the end teach me more than school ever would. Once through those doors, I was independent.

As a kid I was very creative. The best moments of childhood are memories of me in my room, probably talking to myself, as I became the commander of a large army or the conductor of a great symphony as I flailed my arms back and forth, feeling the imaginary music within the depths of my soul. For me, friends were just a bonus, not a necessity, since I had always been just fine creating magical worlds and illusions on my own.

Being social, I was excited at the possibility of making new friends. Once inside those preschool walls, I made my first real friend of my own. We shared our animal crackers during snacktime, whispered through our naptime, and quickly became confidants once the initial excitement blew over and we decided we missed our mommies.

At the end of the day my mother came to pick me up. I grabbed her hand and proudly introduced her to my "best friend." And then it happened. In the few moments she left me to go speak to the teacher, I became tainted.

"That can't be your mom," my previous confidant blurted nonchalantly. "She's White."

I said not a word of the incident to my mother. But as the next morning passed as quickly as it came, I was beginning to become upset at the idea of not yet proving my relationship with my mother to the girl. That was until we were able to paint.

I watched as the other children began their finger-painting portraits. Most of the colors cluttered their hair and clothes rather than the paper itself. Reaching for a bowl, I snatched the black container and fastened my small fingers around its handle. The paint passed as tar as its thick contents consumed my bowl. Reaching for the white paint, I copied my previous motions as I blended the two colors to form one.

"Black and white makes gray, Heather," my friend snapped. I just smiled and began to stir, not even acknowledging her. I became a mad scientist as I threw myself into my work. The noisy room grew silent as I stirred vigorously and bit my lip while waiting for my master plan to unfold.

"Heather," my teacher now started in, unsure of what to do with the situation, "black and white does make gray, sweetheart."

Tears began to stain my cheeks as I stared at the deep gray sky that sat on my table. For an hour I sat, refusing to break my gaze. Not a muscle in my body moved, besides the hand that just kept stirring. As parents began to collect their children, I finally closed the eyes that had for so long never been open at all.

Then my mother came. Compressing me into a tiny ball, I collapsed in her arms. I begged her to never bring me back to this place; never again could I show myself to these people who had stolen my mommy from me.

At home I told my mom of the terrorizing ordeal I had faced all on my own. I could see in her eyes the agony she felt at not being able to save me, as she always had done in the past.

"You can't paint people," she said, as she began the speech that would explain that skin and paint are two separate entities.

"How do I prove to the kids at school that you are my mom?" I asked her.

"Well," she began, "you just look them in the eyes and tell them, 'Because I said so.'"

When I told this story to my kids at camp a few summers ago, it hit me in a completely new light. How often do you think Satan approaches God saying, "They aren't Yours! Look at them! They are dark and dirty, and You are white as snow. Didn't You see Heather sin last night after she 'prayed' for forgiveness? Didn't You see her lie, cheat, and hurt all those people's feelings? She can't be Yours! She looks nothing like You!"

And then I'm sure that God just smiles. "Trust Me," He says while shaking His head, "she's Mine. They're all Mine." And then He raises His nail-scarred hands, looks the devil right in the eyes, and says, "Because I said so."

In him we have redemption through his blood,
the forgiveness of sins, in accordance with the riches of God's grace.
—Ephesians 1:7

Chapter 9

Expelled

To understand your parents' love you must raise children yourself.
—Chinese proverb

I'll never say that I was the easiest child to parent. I can say that without a doubt the Holy Spirit has been working on me tirelessly, and every day I think I'm doing a little better at becoming less like me and more like Him. It's been a full-time job. God has been especially patient with me, and I am grateful for that. Another thing I am sincerely grateful for are my parents. I don't think I've ever been a terrible kid, but I do think there have been characteristics of me that have put their love to the test. I will say this in defense of myself: I have always been very inclined to deeply respect my family and their authority over me. I was never that kid that disrespected my parents or thought little of them. I just always had a strong will of my own, and sometimes that will led me into things I shouldn't have been in.

Most teenage girls wouldn't be caught dead hanging out with their parents. I very much enjoyed the company of mine. If they were going to dinner, I wanted to be invited. I think they are funny. I like their jokes and their view on life. I never went through a phase when they were "uncool." On many occasions I would ditch my friends because I was having fun staying home and talking and just hanging out with my family. I understand that most teenage girls, however, are not like this. I loved, and still love, my parents deeply. However, I had other ways of being disruptive.

For instance, the elementary school I attended developed a disciplinary process called citations. If a student did something a teacher thought was insubordinate, they would issue a citation saying what the student did wrong, and both student and teacher had to sign it. When my stay at that institution had ended, my parents received a large box filled to the brim with all the citations I had collected during my years there. With them came a variety of different things the teachers felt I had done wrong: I skipped class, cheated on math homework, talked during quiet time. I wasn't a perfect child, but looking back, I would hardly deem myself a threat to the school system. Unfortunately for me, that's exactly what the school system decided; they wouldn't necessarily expel me, but strongly recommended that my parents relocate me to a different school. What they said pretty much was "Relocate her before you have to."

For a 12-year-old girl who had attended the same small church school since first grade, this was quite the trauma. All my friends were there. I by no means was a saint, but I was hardly a villain, either. I was 12 and opinionated. I was hyper and had a way with words. I think more than anything they wanted to squelch my embers out before they caught fire with the other kids.

I can remember when the principal, whom I had grown to know very well during my years there, pulled me into his office, my second home, for one of our heart-to-hearts. "Heather, one bad peach can spoil the whole bunch," he said. Now, I have no qualms with that principal to this day. I actually felt as though he was always fair and dealt with me kindly. His words, however, still ring in my ears. By the time I was in eighth grade I truly believed I was a "bad peach." I didn't care anymore what I did, because I thought I was rotten. I became extremely depressed and lost a lot of self-worth. They said I was bad, so I became bad and didn't care anymore how my actions affected anyone else. It got so grueling that I started hearing my name over the PA system during the morning announcements to come to the principal's office. I think the goal was to separate the bad peach from the rest of the crate so that I couldn't contaminate them.

It was my time there that further connected me to writing. I'd sit in the principal's office and write these poems about how I was feeling. I kept a book of those poems and still have it somewhere in my old room at my parents' house. It was the only time in my life that I felt incredibly misunderstood and worthless. I tried to be nonchalant when the other kids would make light of all the hours I spent in the office. I didn't tell them or let them see how much it actually was affecting me.

By the time I was asked to leave the school I felt like such a burden on everyone that I even had a few thoughts of suicide. Why would anyone want someone so bad around? I genuinely started to think that I was useless. I remember being terrified to tell my mother when she came to pick me up from school that she couldn't bring me back the next day. She pulled into the parking circle, and as I jumped into the car I contemplated never telling her. I thought that just maybe I could allow her to continue packing me sandwiches in my lunch box and I could hang out behind the school all day until she arrived to take me home. I couldn't hold it in, though, and I collapsed into her arms and sobbed, apologizing for being so bad.

"I don't think you're bad at all," she said to me, sincerely checking my face with confusion. She wasn't oblivious to my situation at school, but I don't think she ever thought I would actually get expelled.

To make a long story short, my parents met with the school board and were extremely disappointed with their decision to remove me from the school district. In fact, they were angry. You hear of kids getting expelled for drugs, fights, or vandalism, but talking? I think a few of the teachers just wanted me out of their hair. I even had one citation for "vandalism of school property" because I got in trouble for leaning back in my chair. I don't mean to make a mountain out of a molehill now because obviously I turned out just fine, and I very much believe in the power of a Christian education, but I do worry a bit about other students who may have felt like I did. Luckily, I had incredible parents who could lift me up when I felt lifeless, but had I not, I am not sure the ending would have been the same.

After being asked to relocate, my parents enrolled me in public school. I was honestly terrified because it was half way through my eighth-grade year and I didn't know anyone. Plus, in church school you have terrible ideas of what those public school children must be like. I was beyond afraid to have my first day there. Once in public school, however, I found out that I wasn't bad at all. I was rambunctious, I was strong-willed, but I wasn't bad. Throughout my four years in public education I became the newspaper and yearbook editor, I was on the homecoming court, I was the cheerleading captain, and I don't think I ever got in trouble once.

I even represented my school, and town as first runner-up to Miss Berrien Springs in the school's scholarship pageant. They had bad kids in public school, real fish to fry, so fortunately for me I was off the radar. I remember at the end of my eighth-grade year there, during a parent-teacher conference, my science teacher told my parents, "Heather is a very unique and creative child. Tell the church school they can send us more of their bad kids anytime."

The point of this story isn't to bash Christian education. I will without a doubt send my kids to a Christian school, and still find it to be a ministry that I often give my tithes and offerings to help fund. My experience is clearly not everyone's experience. I tell you this story because of how it shaped my life. I was made to believe that I was a bad kid; a kid that I internalized the world would be better without. I was lucky to have parents that loved me dearly. They believed in me and supported me to the end. Without their support I sometimes wonder who, or where, I would be now. My world told me I was bad, but my parents saw the good in me. The citations were irrelevant to them. They knew my heart and became a rock for me in a time in my life when I felt severely misunderstood.

I think that's vitally important for why God often compares His relationship with us to that of a parent-child relationship. Take it from me, God knows you. He'll tell you when you're wrong, but He doesn't hold anything against you. He will never kick you out. Only you can "relocate" yourself from His grace. Only you can grieve Him or separate yourself from His compassionate care.

When you feel like no one understands you, take heart that Christ does. He sees you as only a parent can see their child—with love and mercy. No, it doesn't matter how many citations the devil brings to your trial. He can tally them up till he is blue in the face. God doesn't care about what you've done; He cares about what you will do. He lives in the present, not the past, yet can see the future. Besides, in one way or another we're all bad. We're all sinful and rotten and have fallen short of the glory of God. We don't deserve it, but He keeps loving us anyway. I think Jesus is the only man I know who is proud to have purchased a crate of "bad peaches."

For God so loved the world that he gave his one and only Son,
that whoever believes in him shall not perish but have eternal life.
—John 3:16

Chapter 10

From Peaks to Valleys

It is a mistake to suppose that men succeed through success;
they much oftener succeed through failures.
Precept, study, advice, and example
could never have taught them so well as failure has done.
—Samuel Smiles

I've had God slam doors I spent years prying open. I've seen Him take away some of the biggest things I held dear. I've seen Him let me fail.

I like to think I am a talented and creative person. I have dreams, some small, others large, and many unspeakable. I also have some that stay knotted deep within the belly of my soul, a pact between God and me that I've never vocalized. I also believe in the power of prayer. All it takes is a mustard seed, right? The thing about life is we don't have any control over it. There's no way to "plan" through a sudden passing of a friend, no way to "prepare" for the end of a meaningful relationship, and no way to tell a 5-year-old to "put their best foot forward" during their parents' divorce, because that's life. People, relationships, and dreams die.

So we try to create sayings or phrases that by all means "sound good" in our heads. We just "put our best foot forward," remember to "dance in the rain," tell each other that "tomorrow's another day," and we can walk away usually feeling somewhat useful; pat ourselves on the back for being the rope in someone's ditch. That is until we are the ones in need of the saving. Then words aren't enough. Then we start blaming every person possible for causing our setback, and usually every person but ourselves.

When I was in the fourth grade, I wanted to be a singer. I wrote songs and hummed melodies as if I were to be signed to a major record label in between math class and recess. I was dedicated to my mission. I put in several hours of practice, set up imaginary concerts, and pleaded with God that if He could just give me the opportunity, I'd sing my heart out, and to Christian music, too.

Finally my moment came (as much as it can, anyway, for a 10-year-old girl still mastering long division). A group of my friends started a band. They practiced at recess and lunch, and, luckily for me, were in need of a fourth member. Understandably, I was up for the challenge. After all, this was my 15 minutes, my shining hour, the opening of my curtain. I had arrived. And so I sang to them as best as I could. I let my spirit take me away as I let loose crescendos and put my alto voice in soprano ranges. I belted notes I didn't even know I was capable of, all the while praying to God to hold me together.

When I concluded, my 10- and 11-year-old comrades not only expressed to me that I was incredibly out of tune; they also made sure I heard, through their laughter, that I would never be a singer, not even in a band of fourth graders. They did, however, like the song I had written, and asked for permission to sing it when they produced their first album.

It wasn't the first time I had watched a dream die, and it wouldn't be the last. Every year I am stunned at how many times one person can be rejected and still get out of bed in the morning. Sometimes I wonder if rejection is a necessary ingredient in God's plan for my life, because I sure have seen a lot of it. I am not saying that sarcastically, either. I think life has a road map, and I wonder if it is important, that wherever I am to end up at the end of this journey, for rejection and failure to have been a molding element in order for me to get there successfully. I've really learned how to deal with disappointment. It's taught me to quit making so many plans for myself, because God's plans typically never coincide with mine, and He is not shy about letting me know it.

On the flip side, He has given me so many blessings that I never would have even thought of for myself. Those are my favorite moments, when He presents the reason after a huge devastation. He conjures up something so much bigger and better than you would have ever dreamed of. In those moments He takes my breath away. Every time is the first time, and tears well up in my eyes and I am forced to praise His name for being the orchestrator and planner of my life. I am smiling as I type this because just yesterday He provided me with one of these moments. My knees literally got weak. Anyone who says that there is not a God has never invited Him to play an active role in their life, because if there is one thing I know for sure, it's that God will intercede on your behalf if you will only step aside.

Well, it's been 10 years since my audition for a girls' group, and I'm still not a singer. I'm still not the fourth member of anybody's band and I would also probably still get laughed at if I tried to crescendo. I had a dream, with all the right intentions and all the right prayers, die that day. I watched God let me fail.

It was probably the next day that I realized, however, that though my voice was bad, my song wasn't. I was a good writer, and I decided that maybe that was something I could work with. Maybe If I had made the band that day I wouldn't have spent the next 10 years of my life sharpening my pencils to capture my words.

I may never become a Pulitzer Prize-winning author. I may never be editor of a magazine or publish a world-renowned novel. I may never change the world of journalism or write a hit song. I may even be forced to watch dumbfounded as more of my dreams break to pieces in the grips of my hands, because as I learned that day on the playground, that's life—peaks and valleys. No matter how insensitive it may sound through the tears in my eyes, sometimes all you really can do is "hit the ground running."

I want to provide you with a verse that God used to speak to me one day when I was racked with, yet again, rejection. Jesus said in John 16:20-24, "'Very truly I tell you, you will weep and mourn while the world rejoices. You will grieve, but your grief will turn to joy. A woman giving birth to a child has pain because her time has come; but when her baby is born she forgets the anguish because of her joy that a child is born into the world. So with you: Now is your time of grief, but I will see you again and you will rejoice, and no one will take away your joy. In that day you will no longer ask me anything. Very truly I tell you, my Father will give you whatever you ask in my name. Until now you have not asked for anything in my name. Ask and you will receive, and your joy will be complete.'"

I was crying one day after receiving some unexpected news, and I did something I rarely do anymore: I prayed and asked God to speak to me, and simply opened my Bible. My eyes landed on John 16:20-24, and I knew Christ was taking the time to comfort me. Now may be your time to grieve, but take heart. If you hold true to your faith in Christ, a time is coming when you will again have joy, and no one will be able to take it away from you! God, the same God that created this universe and laid the blueprint for the human body down to our molecular cells, has a plan for you.

Sometimes our dreams for our lives aren't in harmony with God's master plan. Sometimes dreams need to die so others can find breath. Sometimes God lets us fail so the taste is sweeter when we win. Sometimes it's in the valley where we gain the strength to find the peak.

Therefore, since we have a great high priest who has ascended into heaven,
Jesus the Son of God, let us hold firmly to the faith we profess.
For we do not have a high priest who is unable to empathize with our
weaknesses, but we have one who has been tempted in every way,
just as we are—yet he did not sin. Let us then approach God's throne of
grace with confidence, so that we may receive mercy and find grace to help
us in our time of need.
—Hebrews 4:14-16

Chapter 11

Ginger and Cinnamon

Anger is never without a reason, but seldom with a good one.
—Benjamin Franklin

One thing I have always found comical is how confident we are in ourselves when we do something extraordinary. Anytime we do something great that deserves some sort of praise, we are the ones who accomplished it. The good things that happen in life are always one of our own accords. Ironically, as soon as something goes wrong, God becomes the one who has caused this tragic twist in events. The second a lemon comes flying at us we curse God for putting us in these terrible predicaments.

I learned at a young age that as humans, in life, we actually control nothing but our attitudes. We can determine only how we handle the situation in front of us; not ever do we have much control over the situation itself.

I found this out quickly because of my first hamster named Cinnamon. Mom and Dad bought one for both Natasha (my sister) and me. My sister named hers Ginger. They were sister hamsters, and though I couldn't have been much older than 6, I loved Cinnamon (my hamster) as if I had given birth to her myself. She was awfully pretty and had a cinnamon-tinted brown coat of fur that usually smelled like wood and lettuce, an aroma I had grown to truly appreciate.

One day I went to check on Cinnamon in her cage, as I often did when I returned home from hopscotch. I had not prepared myself for what I was about to see, though I'm not sure I could have even with prior knowledge. I flipped on my light switch and strolled over to her cage, expecting to see her running on that little running wheel on which she spent most of her time enjoying herself. As I pressed my face to the glass I saw that she was indeed on her wheel, but not running, not even moving. She was dead, stiff as a board.

I mourned the loss of Cinnamon. She had grown to be very important to me, and the loss of her hurt me immensely. My sorrow, however, would quickly turn to anger when I'd see my sister Natasha still playing with Ginger. Her hamster was still very much alive and very much happy.

I had always questioned whether or not she had even truly appreciated her hamster. She never held her quite as tight as I had held Cinnamon. She never sang Ginger to sleep or took her for walks around the house in that little plastic ball she'd scurry about in. My sister played with the neighbors, watched TV, and rode her bike. She was ambivalent to Ginger's life. She always wanted a dog. The hamster was nice, but a dog was what she really wanted. Not me. I'd like a dog, but it didn't stop me from loving Cinnamon. I am certain that if you asked her now, she would have no idea what Ginger smelled like, or even remember that she had ever existed. Had Ginger died, I was sure Tasha would have choked out one tear before going back to her Super Nintendo unscathed. She didn't know what it took to be a mother as I did, so why did Cinnamon die and Ginger live?

There were times I could have strangled Ginger when I saw her little brown coat of fur. Thank God I didn't. I decided that Cinnamon's death was just out of my control, and if I couldn't bring her back, the least I could do was be happy for her sister, even if at the moment I wasn't that happy for mine.

You see, life is all about attitude, and we technically control nothing but that. So whatever happened last year that left you angry, hurt, or empty, try to leave it in the past and look toward a new beginning. It's a completely blank day now, and the only person who can fill in your pages is you. Besides, you can't keep persecuting God for your misfortunes without first sifting through all the miraculous things that "you've done" lately and giving Him credit.

Someone once told me, "Don't pray when the rain falls if you weren't praying when the sun was shining." I wouldn't take it that far. I'm not sure God's that picky. He is just like a parent in that way. He doesn't care if you haven't called for two years; He is just ecstatic that you are calling now. Today, be thankful. Pray without ceasing. Make God your friend and catch Him up on your life from your perspective. Take a step back from your life and think about everything that He has done instead of what He hasn't done that you wanted Him to. I had to learn the hard way that God doesn't work on your timetable, but He definitely has a plan.

I don't know why Cinnamon died. Sometimes in life you lose something, and later it all makes sense as to why it was necessary that you lost it. Sometimes, however, things just never add up. I had to learn that if I believe

God is good, I can't keep questioning His goodness. I have to simply take Him at His word. Psalm 107:1 says, "Give thanks to the Lord, for he is good; his love endures forever." God is wisdom, He is knowledge, He is love, and He is good. Even when life happens beyond my understanding I have to just remember that God is who He said He is, so in the end all things will work out toward goodness and glory.

When I get to heaven, I am sure He will fill me in on all the questions that just never seemed to make sense to me. Until then, I have just learned to stop questioning Him. The only question I need to ask is "Heather, do you truly believe that God is good?" If my answer is yes, then I can't worry anymore about what I am not seeing. I just have to trust that indeed there is something I am not seeing. If I quit believing that God is good, then I have bigger issues than just whatever ailment I am currently dealing with. I have just completely switched my entire worldview. If God is not good, then the way I view the world, my place in the world, and everything else about life also is going to need to be adjusted.

Fortunately, God is good. I don't really need much convincing on that, because there are enough times in my life when I have already seen Him prove it. The only person who wants you to dwell on the things we cannot change is the devil. And the devil knows that God is good; he just doesn't want us to, because misery loves company.

Sometimes a lot can go wrong. Things can turn on the drop of a hat and leave you completely dumbfounded. Regardless of what's going on in your life, take a second and ponder all the good God has done for you. If that seems like too much right now, it's OK; I am also a fan of baby steps. In life, no matter what, there is always an opportunity for growth. If nothing else, at the very least, take a moment to do what I could not do when I was 6 years old and mourning the loss of Cinnamon. Be better than I was, and be happy for someone else.

I know what it is to be in need, and I know what it is to have plenty.
I have learned the secret of being content in any and every situation,
whether well fed or hungry, whether living in plenty or in want.
—Philippians 4:12

Chapter 12

Bruises and Mustard Stains

We can do no great things, only small things with great love.
—Mother Teresa

I can fool a lot of people. I can lie, manipulate, and probably trick just about anyone into believing the role I sometimes find myself playing. One thing, however, is certain: I can never fool my father.

I can remember it still. I had come home from college to enjoy a Sabbath dinner with my family when my father noticed a small bruise on the right side of my left arm. It must have been spring, because I was wearing a short-sleeve T-shirt.

"What happened?" he asked me, picking up my arm and bringing the bruise closer to his face so he could examine it.

"I tripped over my shoelaces at track practice," I answered. The story was true. I had even cut my laces to ensure it would never happen again. Being a sprinter and running full speed into a handoff is never good when your laces send you hurdling toward your relay team member and knock you out of the exchange zone. This blatant show of a lack of coordination on my part was far less embarrassing than other demonstrations.

I have a scar on my knee because of a far more memorable incident my freshman year of college. I had developed a crush on one of the older boys on campus. He was slightly a rebel, a trait that, at the time, I admired. He was really passionate and had a way with words, at least to an 18-year-old freshman who had a knack for believing almost any lie an older male on campus could spoon-feed her. You can only imagine my delight when this guy actually took notice of me. Out of all the freshman girls, he spotted me. It was like winning a second-rate, much smaller version of the lottery. I was thrilled.

One day I went to work out in the gym, partly because I was on the track team and it was mandatory to do nighttime exercises, and partly because I knew he would be there. Not only was I charmed by this boy; I was also displaying some slightly stalker-like tendencies I am happy no one noticed . . .

So off to the gym I went to run on the treadmill and hopefully have him spot me. I started my run, and things were going great. He came into the gym (right on time) and saw me running. He came over, gave me a smile, and chatted with me for a bit. I loved the fact that all the girls in there saw this outright display of affection from him to me. Our relationship was progressing beautifully. I was relishing in the thought that all the girls in there would go back to their dorms and probably tell their roommates that they had seen the two of us clearly flirting.

After many coy smiles were exchanged and I had laughed sufficiently at enough of his jokes, he went into the weight room, leaving me to finish my run. My heart was still pounding and I was daydreaming about our possible future together, when suddenly something quite literally yanked me out of my fantasy. My shoelace had somehow gotten caught in the tarp of the treadmill and I was facedown getting skinned alive. Eventually another girl noticed what had happened and came to my rescue and turned off the machine. This was one of the most humiliating experiences of my whole life. My entire track team found out about it and never let me live it down. So naturally, when I tripped yet again, later in the season, this time I wised up and cut those hazardous laces.

The facts on how I had received the bruise my father noticed wasn't what made this particular story memorable. It wasn't that it hurt so bad it's been sketched into my memory like a tattoo on unblemished skin. It wasn't that I was so embarrassed for falling, or that the bruise was so large I couldn't forget it; the bruise was tiny, almost unnoticeable. The reason this memory is so dear to me is simply that my father had noticed anything at all.

I don't know about you, but I have this really terrible characteristic. For the most part, I am completely self-absorbed, one of my many flaws. I know this because every time a friend shows me a picture, my eyes go straight to the only part of the photo I ever really see—myself. It can be littered with a beautiful landscape, a scenic backdrop, or a tan on my best bud only a sun outside of Michigan could produce, and yet the only part of the picture I really pay attention to is myself.

Thank goodness for daddies, fathers who notice a frown when the rest of the world is fooled by its disguise as a smile. As a kid, I understood immediately the impact and symbolism that having Christ as our Father creates. He is our Abba, our Daddy. Christ is the type of Lord I picture sifting through the photo album of our lives and chuckling. Not because of a memory, and not because of some long-standing joke between us and Him, but simply because of the tiny mustard stain right below our left sleeve that we thought no one else would notice.

God sees us. We're transparent before Him. He feels the excitement in our joy and understands the depth of our sorrows. Sometimes I've tried to cover up whatever pain is plaguing me, because I want to stand firm in this picture-perfect Christian form I find myself presenting to everyone else. It's funny because we talk about how no one's perfect, but rarely do we allow others into the imperfections in our own lives. For a long time that was my complaint with Christianity, church, and church people. It all seemed so fake to me. It seemed fake on the outside, and I felt fake on the inside. Countless times I went to church feeling small, and I wondered if anyone else could see me for the con artist I know I've often been. Sometimes I even feel guilty.

I'm lucky, however, because though I may try to fool others with perfection, I can't fool God; and I guess there's freedom in that. Every dirty deed, and every sincere one, He has already seen, and yet still calls me friend. He still comforts me when I'm broken, and still loves me in spite of who I really am. There have been times that I've wondered how many people would still want to read my articles or books, or continue to e-mail me about how I've touched them, if they knew how much I've struggled in the past to get to where I am today. That is one of the reasons 60 percent of our young people are leaving the church. Because they feel it lacks authenticity.

I realized, though, where my error was. I was just going to church and then going home. I went to public school, so I didn't have many church friends, and my Christianity ended when my pew time was up. I felt fake because I loved God but struggled to experience Him daily. I changed all that the first time I entered a small group. The first small group I was in wasn't even really trying to be a small group, but it served the same purpose in my life. I worked at FLAG (Fun Learning About God) camp as a counselor for the first time the summer of 2006. There I met people who were authentic, and I wanted what they had found. We talked honestly about our journey with Christ. We told the truth, removed the masks, and it changed my life.

If you are someone who, like me, struggles to find the authenticity of Christianity, join a small group. One of my professors always says to his class of studying pastors, "You will never complete someone's need for God from the pulpit." Small groups are where embers blaze. It's where, through trust and community, you build open relationships and answer tough questions. If your problem is not genuine authenticity, if you already practice· what you preach, then still join a small group. There will be others who will be connected to Christ, not because of what they've read, but because of what they've seen. Your example could make all the difference. For me it did.

I think Satan tries to create this notion within our minds that if God knew us like he knows us, He would have nothing to do with us. He tries to convince us that we are unworthy, and I guess in many ways he is right. The funny thing, though, is that God knows all this. He knows our ins and outs. He's seen the struggle, watched the war, and gazed as we've completely messed it all up. He knows just how jaded we really are, and still He loves us.

I think it is C. S. Lewis who talks about the beauty of sinners. He explains that with God, the bigger the sinner, the bigger the joy in repentance. I've clung to that picture because I know I must have brought heaven a lot of joy when I really decided to try to be a disciple for Christ. Seriously, I was probably one of heaven's wild cards for a long time. I'm sure the heavenly beings watched me and pulled their hair out. When that personal connection with Jesus Christ really developed in my life, I imagine it was a big celebration with a lot of high-fiving. I've made a lot of mistakes, I have a lot of bruises and stains, but there is joy in repentance.

He has seen me at my worst, and thus appreciates my best like no one else can really fathom, and that's not even the best part. For me, the best part is the Daddy factor. Whether you're like me and have this incredible picture of fatherly love to compare Christ to, or you never had a dad and therefore have had to ask God to really fill that void in your life in a special way, we can all reap the fruit of having a Papa—the kind who loves you for who you are, and knows you when you no longer know yourself.

When the big bad world chews you up and spits you out, He is there to put the Band-Aids on your knees and put you right back in the game. As you dust yourself off and fumble as you try standing back up, He lends you a hand for stability. And right when you think it couldn't get any better than this, He chuckles and points out your mustard stain—that inconsequential little dot right below our left sleeve that we were sure no one else would catch. Because God is all about the small things, such as unimportant, microscopic bruises that only a father would ask about.

As a father has compassion on his children,
so the Lord has compassion on those who fear him.
—Psalm 103:13

Chapter 13

I Made My Daddy Smile

There are no secrets to success.
It is the result of preparation, hard work,
and learning from failure.
—Colin Powell

I was 16 years old and finally allowed to take my driver's test. This was my moment. My sister had been cruising the streets of our town for about three years now, and soon I would be behind that wheel.

My friends and I had all decided what our license plates would read, and we planned to park in a row every morning for high school. H-Diddy would soon be my alias. Before you start judging me, it was 2003 and we were in a Puff Daddy phase at the time, and so it seemed only fitting.

I can remember pulling into the parking lot as if it were yesterday. My father had been helping me practice, and driver's ed was now a part of my past. Today would be all about me creating my future as a licensed Michigan driver.

The car was a 1990-something baby-blue Lincoln Town Car. My friends nicknamed it "The Boat" because of its massive size. Parking can be tough for any 16-year-old, but try learning to park in a boat that doesn't give an inch on either side of the lines. You can forget about parallel parking. I was thoroughly embarrassed about it, but I figured a car was better than sneakers. There comes a point in your teenage years when riding your bike outside of recreational purposes is just embarrassing. Almost all my friends were already driving. Being dropped off by my parents had certainly lost its luster.

I could barely sleep the night before the big driving test. I had already passed the written test, and it was time to have my knowledge put to good use. I had been practicing my driver's license smile in the mirror for weeks now. I could not wait to have those keys in my hand, and I could hardly breathe as my father drove me to the testing site.

The test began almost as abruptly as it ended. I never made it out of the parking lot. I failed the parking section so horrendously that the test administrator said there was no way for me to make up the points.

"That's it for today," she said, looking over at me coldly. My eyes instantly welled up with tears, and I swore to her that if she'd just give me one more chance I could do better. Unfortunately, she was completely unaffected by all my displays of emotion, and informed me that in two weeks I could come back and try again, but that we were done for today.

I cried and collapsed into my dad's arms for at least 15 minutes. I was humiliated. How could I go back to school and look all my friends in the eyes now? How could I show my face in the parking lot with my father still dropping me off? They knew I was scheduled to take the test that day and would certainly all ask to see my new license, the license I didn't have.

I'd like to tell you that it wasn't as bad as I had imagined and that my friends all completely understood, but they didn't. The guys we hung out with made fun of me until I graduated, and to this day my friends still whisper behind my back that I'm a terrible driver. In my senior speech class, about two years post-license, a guy friend of mine did his entire speech on how women are terrible drivers and cited me as his example. I am not a terrible driver; yet this stigma has followed me ever since that day. I could be a chauffeur for a living and it wouldn't have changed a thing. The damage was done the second the testing instructor directed me to get out of the car prematurely.

My father, however, believed in me. He took me out every day after school and we practiced parking. It reminded me of the times I was a kid and he'd put his foot on the pedal in a parking lot and let me steer. I could honestly tell that he had felt my pain the day I was rejected at the driving center, and he made it his mission to help me succeed. He made time for me almost every afternoon after school—20 to 30 minutes to drive around looking for different parking scenarios.

I waited a few months before I took the test again. I couldn't bear the thought of adding insult to injury if the instructor sent me home empty-handed twice. Once the second time to take the test rolled around and the administrator got in the passenger seat, I instantly had flashbacks. I had to swallow hard and put the past in the past. She gave me a nod that meant it was time to go, and I began the test all over again, and this time I passed.

The funny thing is it isn't her writing up my paperwork that I remember most fondly. It isn't getting the keys to my first car, signing my name on my license at the DMV, or flashing that winning smile for the camera that I had spent months practicing. The best memory I have of that entire experience is watching my dad out of the rearview mirror when the parallel parking section was complete. He was hiding behind an old bus, watching me knock over a cone or two with that boat of a Lincoln Town Car.

I could feel the sweat build up on my palms as the pressure of his presence consumed me. And then, as I turned the wheel and slid that blue tugboat into its designated area, I saw him do it. As if someone had just told him he had become an overnight billionaire, he flew off his feet and into the air. He clapped his hands, then raised his fist to the sky as if he'd just won the Boston Marathon. He was genuinely happy for me, and my mind has protected that memory of my daddy filled with such joy ever since.

Sometimes now I'll feel like a loser, like I'm a 16-year-old girl again and just failed my first driver's test, like I can't catch a break, or like I'm so far away from my goals that I might as well leave them where they are and move on. Sometimes I lose faith in myself.

It's in those moments that I'll reach back into my mind and pull out that perfectly timeless memory of my father with this incredible smile on his face all because I had succeeded. And then I realize that if my earthly father can be that enthralled because I finally passed my driver's test, how much bigger will be the smile on my heavenly Father's face when I persevere in His mission for my life?

God is good. Sometimes we say that but forget to believe it. Jesus said if the parents who raised us truly want the best for us, how much more can we expect from Him? If the daddy who created my body could believe in me, then how much stronger would be the faith of my Father who created my soul? Jesus asks us to have faith in Him, and that should really be the easy part. It's His role of having faith in us that is constantly being tested. Yes, God is good. So good that He sends us smiles from fathers to remind us of the beams exploding from the Son.

The Spirit you received does not make you slaves, . . .
rather, the Spirit you received brought about your adoption to sonship.
And by him we cry, "Abba, Father."
—Romans 8:15

Chapter 14

I Met Christ at Breakfast

Friendship is unnecessary, like philosophy, like art. . . .
It has no survival value;
rather it is one of those things that give value to survival.
—C. S. Lewis

I had breakfast in the café with a friend of mine. I didn't have to be awake yet, but I was. I would have my first chemistry exam in about two hours and, other than cramming scientific information, I also believe in the power of a good breakfast to start my day. Soon, however, I was about to become intensely aware of another power I had forgotten—prayer.

Chemistry was one of the hardest undergraduate courses I ever took. I hired a tutor, and had it not been for him, I'm still not sure I wouldn't be in a lecture hall somewhere hoping that things could be different this time around. Chemistry has a lot of elements that I am not good at. It has science, which isn't one of my strong points, coupled with mathlike equations that make my eyes water on contact. My hate for math started in about the eighth grade when the foreign-exchange student I had hired to complete all my homework ratted me out to the principal and math teacher. Suddenly I was on my own, and it wasn't pretty. I was much older now, and having learned from my childhood errors, I, in a legit manner, hired a tutor, who did not actually do my homework, but sat with me in the library basement for hours until I understood the principles. Note here: When you cheat, you really are only cheating yourself.

Chemistry was a bit easier for me than math because some words were involved. I could read this stuff, and that helped somewhat. Also, chemistry tests typically had some short answers, and explaining things through written words is one of my better features. I can remember every time I took a chemistry exam, I was the very last student left in a lecture hall of about 75 people. The professor would kindly invite me to his office to finish my exam. I liked to take my time with chemistry. As any good chemist, I recognized that this was an art that should not be rushed. All in all, chemistry was a mixed bag for me, filled with highs and lows.

As I was eating my breakfast, an old friend approached and asked if she could take a seat. Her name was Sylvi Gonzalez, and not only was she beautiful, well spoken, and intelligent—she was also an authentic Christian. I hadn't been able to connect with Sylvi in a while, and so when she sat next to me I began pouring my heart out to her. I told her everything that was going wrong in my life, which was more than just the chemistry exam. I talked to her about my panic as graduation was coming up, about the relationship I was in at the time, and even my fears that I would never become the person I felt God had created me to be. We also talked about the most imminent problem, that being this test for this general-level chemistry class, which I had brilliantly left until my last semester of undergrad to take. Next note here: DON'T DO THAT! Even though I had studied for hours upon hours and met with my personal tutor for months, I still wasn't expecting to reap any fruit from my labor.

I went on and on, telling her all these things, allowing my thoughts and emotions to be spilled onto her very inviting and caring ears. I told her everything, and as I spoke, monopolizing most of the conversation, I didn't expect anything more from her than just her attention. There is such beauty and craftsmanship in the art of listening. I never really thought to myself, *What if Sylvi is also having a rough day? What if she needs someone to confide in?* If she did, she never said so. She just smiled, nodded, and gave a few tidbits of advice wherever she could.

At the end of our conversation I gave her a hug and started clearing the leftovers back onto my tray as I got up to leave. I stood, feeling lighter after our heart-to-heart, but still uneasy. As I turned to walk away, she grabbed my hand and performed the greatest act of love I had received in a random passing in quite some time. She asked if she could pray for me, and she was genuine.

I am usually the type of person who is uncomfortable in group prayer. I typically don't pray with others, because all of a sudden I feel a need to try to be "extra holy." There again, you see this lack of authenticity. You know what I mean. You say a few extra lines you probably wouldn't have had it been just you praying alone. Suddenly you find yourself making a sermon out of a prayer, and if something good comes out of your mouth you open your eyes a bit just to make sure those who are around got all of that. In order to get rid of this temptation, I rarely volunteer to pray publicly. Not because I have nothing to say, but because I fear getting carried away all because I feel as though that is how I am supposed to be praying. The last thing I want is to pray insincerely.

This was not Sylvi's issue. I could tell it was easy for her: not even a second thought, just an action she would have performed for anyone. Her words were simple too. No drawn-on narratives to hear the sound of her own voice, no hypocrisy, no "fake holiness." Just a simple prayer to the Man it was obvious she knew so well, interceding for me.

The rest of the day I was touched. I still wasn't sure if I would ace my chemistry test, but all of a sudden it didn't matter. I had found peace in the prayer of a friend. I went into the exam room feeling free of worry, which so often can strap onto our backs so heavily that it's all we can do just to stand. She took that burden from me, and she made it look simple.

I'm still unsure whether I will be able to become exactly who God created me to be, though I have peace that every day I may be stumbling closer. I didn't get any sudden answers or instant clarification that morning, but I did learn something else. I learned how helpful one can be to someone else's bad day by lending their ears to listen and their mouth to do nothing but say a simple prayer for them.

I'm almost positive that Sylvi Gonzalez doesn't remember having breakfast with me that morning. I haven't seen or heard from her in a couple years now. All I know is that she went on to study law somewhere. (At least that was her plan after graduation.) Wherever she is, I am sure she is still touching people with her genuine brand of Christianity. She taught me that day that one of the most honorable things I can do for someone is intercede for them through prayer. It sounds so easy that I wonder why I haven't done more of it. Ever since that breakfast with Sylvi, I never miss a chance to ask someone if I can say a quick prayer with them while they try and get through a bad day. No drawn-out narratives, no insincere words, and definitely no "fake holiness." I just think of Sylvi and I try to pass along to someone else the same peace she gave me.

I got an A– in chemistry. I'm not sure if it was all that studying, worrying, tutoring, or a simple prayer at breakfast that contributed to this minor success in my life. All I know is that it was the sweetest kind of success, the kind you have to work for. I never had to take chemistry again, though I would like to say "Thanks" to Dr. Nowack, who was kind enough to allow me not just the time I needed to take his tricky exams, but the use of his office. When the stampede of students scheduled to be in that classroom the following period tramped in, he could have told me that was it, shut off the lights, and went about his day.

Instead, he'd smile and say, "Well, I am going to my office; you're welcome to finish there if you'd like." And with that he'd collect his materials and we would be off. Each time he said it as if it were the first time, as if this weren't our routine, and as if by next exam day I wouldn't need the same treatment. It was a simple statement and gesture of kindness that I never overlooked. In fact, it is the reason I now do the same thing for my students who may also be overthinking a multiple-choice question.

Jesus told His disciples that if they had faith they could move mountains. I don't think He was talking symbolically here, either, because we are talking about a Man that curses a fig tree and it instantly withers. This is God. And if there's one thing I do know for certain it is that with God all things are possible, and usually I'm not even trying to move any mountains, just pass chemistry.

Pray with someone who may need it today. Take 10 seconds to say a prayer for someone else. No false pretenses, no double standard, no "fake holiness," or lack of authenticity, just pure sincerity. Sylvi's random act of faith ignited my love for Jesus Christ and His precious people; people so precious that they'd take the time to stand before God's throne with no thoughts of themselves, just a request for a friend. It doesn't get any closer to Christlike than that. No, I wasn't expecting it, nor did it ever really cross my mind that dawn as I left my home with jumbled-up chemistry notes and a mind full of uncertainty, but I met Christ at breakfast that morning, and now I want to introduce Him to someone else.

My command is this: Love each other as I have loved you.
Greater love has no one than this: to lay down one's life for one's friends.
You are my friends if you do what I command. I no longer call you servants,
because a servant does not know his master's business.
Instead, I have called you friends, for everything that I learned from my
Father I have made known to you.
—John 15:12-15

Chapter 15

Love in Action

Sometimes the heart sees what is invisible to the eyes.
—H. Jackson Brown, Jr.

It took me a while to write this down. I don't want to be a hypocrite, bashing other people's sins when I know I have a drawer full of my own. After all, remove the plank from your own eye before commenting on the speck in someone else's, right? However, I don't believe that this means that we never address issues that we know fellow peers may be struggling with. The following is not a bashing on a sin that some may be struggling with— it's simply an attempt to call it to your attention. Do with it what you want.

I could sit here and list for you many issues that I have or am currently struggling with. I know I may sound like a broken record at this point, but it's intentional. I am not perfect, I do not want to be confused for perfect, and actually I have found peace in who I am and where I am in my life. I can honestly say that every single day during my worship I ask God to give me just a little bit more of His Spirit today than yesterday. I'm not comfortable letting our relationship sit unchanged. I want to get this thing called Christianity down right; I just know that I'm still not there.

A very good friend of mine called me this past summer and asked me to give her a verse in the Bible that explicitly says that sex before marriage is wrong. She said she knew it was, but her boyfriend said it wasn't actually written in the Word, and she couldn't think of a verse that said it. She knew that I am an avid highlighter. I highlight many verses in the Bible that I think I will need to come back to one day.

The first thing I thought of when she called was Ezekiel. God called Ezekiel to be a watchman for Israel, and I believe He similarly calls us to be watchmen for one another. In the past I have not been that great at doing this. I tend to go with the whole "speak when spoken to" concept in regard to sin. If someone asks for my opinion, I will give it; otherwise I keep my mouth shut. Once I read this verse, though, I felt a burden.

I had heard a quote from novelist Elie Wiesel that said, "I swore never to be silent whenever and wherever human beings endure suffering and humiliation. We must always take sides. Neutrality helps the oppressor, never the victim. Silence encourages the tormentor, never the tormented." And I wondered if our silence on important issues with one another encourages Satan.

I have learned, though, that when it's done correctly and in love, you can be a watchman for your peer without being offensive. I have met great Christian friends who were able to hold me accountable without making me feel judged. It's a delicate line to walk, but I think we have to learn how to maneuver it. I think the best advice on how to do this tactfully is to ask yourself, "Do I actually love the person I want to confront about some issue?" If you do, then proceed to confront them with that same love. If you do not, then it probably is not your place. The best way to address these issues, in my opinion, is through the connection of a true and genuine relationship.

Ezekiel 3:20 says this about being a watchman: "Again, when a righteous person turns from their righteousness and does evil, and I put a stumbling block before them, they will die. Since you did not warn them, they will die for their sin. The righteous things that person did will not be remembered, and I will hold you accountable for their blood." This is what made me gulp for air—if you know your friend or loved one is doing something and you don't find a tactful way in love to bring it to their attention, you will be held accountable for that sin as well. That is powerful.

Verse 21 continues: "But if you do warn the righteous person not to sin and they do not sin, they will surely live because they took warning, and you will have saved yourself." After reading these words, I realized again why it is so important not to just be a Christian alone, but to be a Christian in community. The disciples didn't just keep what Jesus had done for them all to themselves; they went out with fire and did their best to set in motion this blaze of true Christian brotherhood and community.

So with this in mind, to answer my friend's question on verses dealing with sexual immorality, I gave her 1 Corinthians 6:18, which says, "Flee from sexual immorality. All other sins a person commits are outside the body, but whoever sins sexually, sins against their own body." This is a strong statement when you use the concept of *sola scriptura*, which says to compare scripture with scripture. If your body is a temple, you are committing a sin against the temple of God.

I also showed her 1 Corinthians 6:9: "Do you not know that wrongdoers will not inherit the kingdom of God? Do not be deceived: Neither the sexually immoral nor idolaters nor adulterers nor men who have sex with men . . . will inherit the kingdom of God." People would like to edit this one a bit, clean it up so that it fits well with our friends and our lifestyles. I love how it says, "Do not be deceived." Satan has totally been working hard to deceive us when it comes to these sexual sins. We think sex is an expression of freedom. Your body, your choice. The media works hard to portray images of men with men, women with women, and even married people who are not sexually "closed-minded" and are confident enough in their own love for one another to allow their partners to have sex outside of the marriage. But do not be deceived.

Second Timothy 2:22 also deals with the importance of purity: "Flee the evil desires of youth and pursue righteousness, faith, love and peace, along with those who call on the Lord out of a pure heart."

The Bible is pretty clear about where it stands on moral issues. We can try to bend it around and twist things to make ourselves more comfortable in our sin, but the Bible is still black and white. People always say, "Well, Jesus hung out with Mary Magdalene, and she was a prostitute." That's true. I've noticed that practically every celebrity who knows probably just this one excerpt from the Bible quotes from her story.

It says in John 8:6, 7, "But Jesus bent down and started to write on the ground with his finger. When they kept on questioning him, he straightened up and said to them, 'Let any one of you who is without sin be the first to throw a stone at her.'"

To me, however, that is not the clutch of Christ's message. The clutch is the fact that He looked at this woman, who was by our standards, and definitely by Jewish law, unclean, and He forgave her. But He did not just forgive her; He was sure to include in John 8:10, 11, "Jesus straightened up and asked her, 'Woman, where are they? Has no one condemned you?' 'No one, sir,' she said. 'Then neither do I condemn you,' Jesus declared."

And here is, in my opinion, the invitation in the story to everyone who reads it. The heart of the story is that there is nothing you can do that can separate you from the love of God. If you really think about what Jesus has just done, He has not only spoken to a woman who has been caught not just in adultery, but also in prostitution; He also defends her. He comforts her. Jesus is not just your judge; He is also your defense attorney. But the next thing He says is the invitation in the story for all who are reading. Verse 11 concludes, "Go now and leave your life of sin."

People usually don't quote that part. The whole "go and sin no more" aspect isn't as useful, and so we edit it. People destroy much of the Bible by editing. I personally believe it is a Book to be read not in quotes, but in its entirety. That is why you cannot even just take our excerpt from Ezekiel and call yourself a watchman when really you are a judgmental, mean tyrant. Read the Bible in its entirety. Understand the concept of love. It is Christ's most adorning characteristic.

We cannot use the Bible to excuse our sin. Being a Christian is all about denying self. Most sins happen because we indulge our appetites with whatever it is we seek, whether that is sex, alcohol, drugs, whatever. If you do those things, the beauty of the salvation story is that Christ does not condemn us, but He does instruct us to go and sin no more. If you aren't ready to take that step with Him, just admit it. There's still hope when you know you're wrong, but when you are blind to it, it's over. I cannot stand when people say, "Well, what you don't know won't hurt you." What you do not know will absolutely hurt you! It could even kill you! Seek knowledge, not ignorance.

At some point in time, if you are simply unwilling to quit doing whatever you are doing that you know is keeping you from being the person Christ really desires that you become, you have to just admit that you refuse to deny self. Please do not give false biblical teachings to other people, excusing whatever it is you are into through excerpted Bible verses.

Jesus Himself said in John 14:23, 24, "Anyone who loves me will obey my teaching. My Father will love them, and we will come to them and make our home with them. Anyone who does not love me will not obey my teaching."

People often say that the only thing you have to do to get to heaven is accept Jesus as your Savior and love Him. They are right, but what does love mean? Jesus clarified that for us, explaining that loving Him means following His teachings, and those who do not follow do not love Him. That verse struck me, and so I highlighted it. I never would have thought that I still didn't truly love God, but by His own words I do not. If you remember one thing out of everything I've said in this entry, please let it be that Christianity is all about denying self on the basis of love. "It is when you die to yourself that you begin to live."

You see, Jesus always loves us, and I'd imagine that it could be hard at times loving people who don't love you back—love in word, maybe, but rarely in action. I've still got a lot of love to learn, and the first step is admitting it.

> *Jesus replied, "Anyone who loves me will obey my teaching.*
> *My Father will love them,*
> *and we will come to them and make our home with them.*
> *Anyone who does not love me will not obey my teaching.*
> *These words you hear are not my own;*
> *they belong to the Father who sent me."*
> *—John 14:23, 24*

Chapter 16

Dotty

My passionate sense of social justice and social responsibility has always contrasted oddly with my pronounced lack of need for direct contact with other human beings and human communities.
—Albert Einstein

In 2007 I was lucky enough to find myself in Dallas, Texas, for the North American Division (NAD) prayer conference entitled Just Claim It. It was in Dallas that I learned three things: Everything really is bigger in Texas, cowboys and saloons are obviously a thing of the past, and the church is moving with a mission.

I was able to spend my time in Dallas learning how to use drama in ministry. I saw quickly that when on stage, everything should be over the top. I felt the Holy Spirit dwell in the walls of our worships, and was fortunate enough to see firsthand that there's a deeply needed call to action in America's nursing homes, reminding our elderly of the power of a Christ who cares for the old just as much as the new.

When we first entered our first nursing home, I could tell that many of the other volunteers were a bit apprehensive. As I told you before, God has been working on me, and I have learned to truly love people. I was excited to meet people who needed some love, and so I jumped right in. Whenever there is an awkward silence and everyone is trying to figure out how to start something, I like to be the first to break the ice. I walked right up to a beautiful woman who was planning on attending our little worship service that day, and I asked how she was doing.

"Just fine," she said a bit coldly.

"I love your nails!" I exclaimed. She had bright-red nail polish on, and if there is one thing I know will melt the heart of any woman, it's a compliment.

"Why, thank you!" she beamed, lifting her hands to me so that I could get a better look. I moved around the room trying to find connections with the other residents. It didn't take long for the other church volunteers to follow my lead.

One woman I met named Dotty asked me for my address. She wanted someone to write to. I gave it to her, and then held her hand for a while. At the end of the program, when I was about to leave, she asked if I would kiss her cheek. I got the impression it had been quite some time since anyone had visited Dotty. My sister is a nurse who works in a nursing home, and I have been told on many occasions some of the more unflattering stories that go on there. Sometimes sanitation for yourself can be hard when dementia sets in. That thought did come into my mind, but I pushed it out. I kissed her, and told her I'd write if she would.

I was amazed by the performances that all the different churches came together to put on in Dallas. I watched students from universities use their God-given gifts to move a room. I watched high school students and youth groups pray for revival. I watched in awe and admiration as I saw my church, our church, seek to find messages that can reach people exactly where they are.

While sitting behind a desk, I spent some time playing secretary for the organization and instructing youth on how to sign up for the various ministries. Outreaches that called 14- through 21-one-year-olds to go out to local juvenile detention centers filled every single possible slot and bus seat. Adults and kids partnering up to knock on the doors of the city of Dallas looking for hearts churning to hear the Word of God was a duty people were begging to fulfill. Ministries teaching people how to use preaching, clowns, puppets, and art, all as an outreach to tug at the hearts of secular society, became a normal sight. I saw Christians practicing Christianity in Dallas, and I was touched.

I think far too often we get too comfortable leaving Christianity to everyone else. We'll just stick to our own, take care of ourselves, and keep it in the family. There are missionaries who sign up to get their hands dirty. No, not me. Isn't it enough I show up and sit in my pew, keep the commandments, hold back from telling my boss what I really think of them, smile at sinners, pay my tithe, and attend a Christian university? You mean to tell me that just when I finally start getting a handle on trying to do all the right things for myself, I have to start leading by example?

Well, I can't speak for everyone, but as far as what I believe, sure. That may be enough. I think you can do all those things and still be able to tuck yourself into bed at night, proud of your accomplishments. I think you do deserve that pat on the back and the kudos you've been longing for. After all, you've earned it. But I also think, and after that week in Dallas was able to see, that while you are sleeping soundly, there's a boy in Minnesota who's contemplating suicide, and a girl in Albuquerque who's grasping at straws to kick her habit. There's a mother in Houston working three jobs to feed her son, and a father in prison who just wants to start over. While we are sleeping, they are fighting, tooth and nail, a battle that's very real and very deadly. And all any of them really needs is to feel someone standing in their corner.

I did get one letter from Dotty. I wrote her back, and never heard anything again. Maybe she forgot about me and our pact that I would write as long as she did. Maybe she had started to write and misplaced my address. Maybe her family started coming again and she didn't need me anymore. Or maybe Dotty died. If she did, I hope that in her loneliness, where one too many relatives simply became too busy to keep their scheduled visit, she found a friend in me. I hope that in the still of the night when human relationship seemed to be but a distant memory, she was able to put her palm to her cheek and feel the warmth of my kiss. I alone cannot make sure that every nursing home resident has a visitor, but then again, if I write this all down, maybe I can.

I felt called to action when I visited the great city of Dallas. I witnessed the supernatural forces that are definitely in a battle. I saw the stone-solid faces of 80- and 90-year-old people smile because someone cared enough to kiss their cheeks. I saw what God is using this generation of young Christians to do, and I saw them fight to save strangers. Now, I don't know about you, but I can't sleep.

We who are strong ought to bear with the failings of the weak
and not to please ourselves.
Each of us should please his neighbors for their good,
to build them up.
—Romans 15:1, 2

Chapter 17

The Cost of Your Heart

*Unless we place our religion and our treasure in the same thing,
religion will always be sacrificed.*
—Epictetus

When I was 18 years old, I entered the Miss Berrien Springs Pageant. I had to win. I had gone through all the rehearsals and practiced for hours alone in front of the mirror. One of my best friends at the time had gotten second runner-up for her town's pageant the year before. She had a lot more money than I did, and let me buy one of her beautiful but terribly expensive dresses to wear. It was perfect. It was ivory and laced with thousands of white and black beads patterned all around it.

Many of the girls wore ball gowns, but mine was tight all the way down to the tiny train that pooled at the bottom. Days before the pageant I would try the dress on and walk around the living room in my heels for my mother and sister, who both insisted that I would make a beautiful queen.

I am pretty sure that every prayer I prayed at night the six months leading up to the pageant was flooded with requests to God about exactly how I wanted this event to go down.

"I don't care if I never win anything else ever again, if I can just be Miss Berrien Springs," I'd say, then shower that with a few pleases before whispering, "Amen."

By the time the night before the pageant finally arrived, I could hardly sleep. I honestly don't think I have had another night racked with that much anticipation since. Every time I started to fall asleep I'd dream about the pageant. I dreamed about what questions the judges would ask me, what facial expression I would make as they placed the crown upon my head, what answers I'd give the town newspapers when they interviewed me about my new title. I tossed and turned most of the night, and finally when it was late enough to get out of bed and make an early breakfast, I did.

I remember going into my parents' bedroom that morning and questioning them, making sure that they had been praying for me to win.

"I never pray for you to win anything," my dad responded. "I just pray that God intercedes in your life."

My father had made his position pretty clear from the beginning. He could care less if I was Miss Berrien Springs. In fact, I always thought he secretly rooted against me. The thought of his youngest daughter prancing around in a pageant didn't rate much on the importance scale to him for the scheme of my life. I'm sure if my personality were different, he may have wanted me to win. The problem was how much he knew I wanted it. I had become completely absorbed into this pageant culture, and that crown would be my treasure.

I had not one friend trying out for the pageant with me. It was open to all the senior girls, and no one in my group of close girlfriends cared to enter. That would have been fine except that this meant I didn't really know any of the other girls involved. They all seemed to be friends with one another; I was kind of an outsider. That was OK, because I didn't really enter to make friends. I entered to win.

The day of the pageant I looked great and did great. I did great in the interview with the judges, great during my walks, great when I made Top Five and did my speech onstage. I had prayed for this religiously, and so I was not surprised that I was doing great—I was only anticipating that moment when I would be crowned.

I can still remember the Top Five question that the moderator asked onstage in front of that large live audience. "Stars shine their light brightly; how do you shine bright in your community?"

It took me but a millisecond to come up with my response. I explained that I shined brightly in numerous ways. When I was old enough to join the newspaper staff, I did, and within a year I became an editor. When I could join the yearbook staff, I did, and I became an editor. When I became a cheerleader, I also did my best, applied myself, and became the cheerleading captain. I told him that whatever I do, I do to the best of my ability, and I believe that this is the best way to shine in your community, by not just doing something, but doing your best at it.

I ended with a thank-you. I flashed a big smile to the audience, and then paused, changed my gaze, and smiled at the three judges, one of which was a previous Miss Michigan U.S.A. I waved, and then turned to leave the stage. The auditorium broke out in applause, and I could hear several of my friends screaming my name and contestant number. It took all I had not to turn back around and fist-pump. I had this thing in the bag, and I knew it.

I was crowned that night—but not as Miss Berrien Springs. I was blindsided when I received first runner-up. Sure, I still opened my eyes bright, smiled big, and pretended this was all I ever wanted, but inside I was furious. Waking up the next morning was painful, as I realized it wasn't a dream and saw that white "First Runner-Up" banner strip hanging over my closet door. I wanted to leap into the air and rip it down. I hadn't entered the pageant to get first runner-up; I'd entered to win. Honestly, it still hurts a bit to talk about. I am over the loss now, but I certainly remember how I felt the morning after.

Reflectively, I am glad I didn't win the pageant. I see that God interceded for me, and I am ecstatic that He cared enough to let me lose. Had I won, I am positive I would have spent the next five years entering every pageant I could, until I made it to Miss America. I'm not being exaggerative here, either. That's my personality. I find something I am good at, and I go all the way with it. I do it till I'm the best. Ask anyone who knows me. I have tunnel vision of the worst kind. I'm like an alligator with something between my jaws; once I've locked on, there's no letting go.

There would have been nothing wrong with me pursuing a career in pageants if that's what God's plan for me had been, but it wasn't. My plan was writing, and there was no time to get distracted. The girl who did win, on the other hand, definitely deserved it. She was a shier girl in high school, and though I entered that pageant not to make any friends, she is to this day one of my very best friends, and I've learned so much from her. She gained a necessary element of confidence from the title, confidence that, if I'm being honest, would probably have worked adversely in my life. There is a fine line between confidence and conceit. I'm glad I wasn't given the chance to walk it.

Now when I want something, I'm not angry when I don't get it. I am completely comfortable sitting back and letting God take the driver's seat. I try to go through doors I know only He has opened, and ask Him to close them when He doesn't need me to be there anymore. I've been fortunate, because I learned to really seek the Holy Spirit's direction when making decisions in my life, and I can't explain to you how much that has changed the course of my future.

I'm sure I'm not the only one here, either. How many of us sit and wedge and pry our own doors open, and then convince ourselves that surely God wants us to be there? Sometimes doors that were never meant to be open are shut. The key is learning how to trust God and seek His guidance in all aspects of decision-making. He has an end goal for you, thus making the routes you take vital to how efficient your trek goes.

I read a Bible verse once that really moved me: "For where your treasure is, there your heart will be also" (Matthew 6:21). It's simple, yet really profound. I had to start asking myself where my treasure was. When I was 18, it was in a metal crown with fake gems on it, and so that's where my heart was. Not with Christ, not with His people, not in love with either Christianity or with His Word. My treasure was not very valuable and thus left my heart aligned with something that, in the big scheme of life, wasn't really important.

Your heart is precious. So choose its company wisely. Your treasure is always somewhere, so it's important that you're honest with yourself about exactly where it lies. Your heart is priceless, so make sure you bind it with treasure that is equally as valuable.

For where your treasure is, there your heart will be also.
—Matthew 6:21

Chapter 18

The Storm

It is not light that we need, but fire;
it is not the gentle shower, but thunder.
We need the storm, the whirlwind, and the earthquake.
—Frederick Douglass

One day one of my nephews became especially dear to my heart. They all are tucked tightly into the pockets of my heart in their own ways. They manage to find their own unique style of pulling on my heartstrings and endearing themselves to me in a fashion much deeper than they can still realize.

This nephew has always been a little smaller than the other boys. He is precious, and though he has grown much since this memory, I am still assured that great things come in small packages.

It was a terrible thunderstorm. One of those storms during which you're sure that if you squeeze your eyes shut tight enough, when you open them your whole house will have moved three feet.

The rain was torrential. I remember, because it was my junior year of high school, and my track team was on its way to the regional meet, where we would try to qualify for state finals. My bus turned around halfway through the trip to go back home. The weather was terrible, and we knew no one would be running that day, no matter how much heart you had.

When I got home, it was intense. Claps of thunder ricocheting loudly, lightning bursting through the dark sky like firecrackers. It was powerful.

I myself love storms, more so when I'm sleeping. Then that howling wind and loud cracks of thunder signal to me that my bed is the absolute perfect place to be. My face curls into a sleepy grin, and those are the mornings that I snooze my alarm clock.

My nephew Jeziah wanted nothing to do with this thunderstorm. He was only 5 at the time, so I couldn't really blame him. He wasn't aware yet of how amazing sleep could be. I was still tricking him into taking naps. My favorite was telling him that we were just going to lie down for a little while, that he could count to 60 thirty times, and then we could get up when he was done. It didn't usually take more than three minutes for him to quit counting and fall asleep beside me. A storm for him seemed to have no upsides.

"Nana," he asked my mother, "why is it so loud out there?"

"That is the thunder that you're hearing," she answered.

"Thunder is scary," he whispered, pressing his face to the glass of our window, watching the tree limbs whip back and forth against their will.

"Nana," he quivered, "look at all the lights in the sky." Suddenly a huge crack whipped, and he flew backward from the window as the muscle in the storm started to flex. He was startled, and so he began to cry.

"What's wrong?" my mom chuckled. "It's just a storm, Jeziah." She pressed him to her chest, but he found no solace in her casual response to this terrifying occurrence. He continued to sob, and as the thunder roared louder, so did he. He took his adorable little-person hands and covered his ears. He made that precious face that little ones make when they wail and their faces scrunch up and crocodile tears flood their cheeks.

My mother went to her notorious rocking chair and cradled him in her arms. "Did you know that when it storms, it is a good thing for the earth? The rain comes down and waters the grass and the trees and all the flowers, and that's how they grow."

My mother has a wonderful knack for making terrifying things seem not so bad. It must be a skill that mothers learn somewhere in between seeing broken arms and bloody knees. You learn how to smile when you want to cry, laugh when you want to scream, and seem brave when your knees are shaking.

"It does?" he said, heaving his chest up and down and trying to swallow back the lump in his throat.

"It does," she said. "The thunder and lightning can be loud and scary, but tomorrow when it's all over, the grass will grow, and so will the plants, trees, and flowers."

He thought about this for a few moments and then hopped off her lap with a sense of urgency. He took a deep breath and then looked everyone in the eyes and said, "I need to go outside."

"Why would you want to go outside?" my sister asked him. "You were just crying like a baby about how scared you were."

My sister has this endearing little quality about herself. Secretly she loves our family dearly. She can write about how great we are, talk to her best pals about how much we all mean to her, but often she'll sling words to our faces that may appear unsympathetic. Rarely is she the one you would want to go to if you're crying. If it's for a good reason, of course, she'll support you and try to right this wrong. But little stuff she slips into her category of spilled milk. Suck it up and keep moving. This tough exterior is surely one of her nuances that we can't imagine living without.

"Please, Auntie," he repeated. "I need to go out there so I can grow."

I was instantly touched. I knew he hated being small, and I found it brilliant that he would hesitate for only a moment before putting himself in a situation he was afraid of if it meant he would grow.

To help paint this picture a little clearer, you should know that my nephew is hardly the first to run into something scary. Like me, he pretends to be no hero. In fact, I remember one time my brother pretended a monster was attacking him in the basement, and his two sons sat on the couch, both unwilling to sacrifice themselves. Not that they didn't care—they did, and they were quick to tell my sister and me that we should help.

After seeing that we weren't budging either, Jaylen, the younger of the two, who was actually 3 at the time, got up and started to head to the basement. He truly believed that a monster was down there, and he got up to face it if it meant protecting his father. It was adorable, because he puffed his chest out, stood up straight, and tried to seem big. Jeziah wished him well, but kept his seat. The kid is brilliant at a lot of things, but facing a fear is not high on his list of priorities.

Some of us can be spiritually small. Some of us, most of us, have times we know we need to grow but are too scared to do the work. We don't want to leave our comfort zones or we're just simply scared of the unknown. God gets it. Storms are scary. They are loud and it rains, and it can really make you shriek. After the storm though, when the clouds part and little streaks of sun come back through your window, you're stronger. You survived the storm, and for that, you have grown. My nephew couldn't stand in the midst of thunder and lightning and grow physically bigger, but he was 5 and willing to. What are you willing to do to grow spiritually? Try facing the storm.

Then they cried out to the Lord in their trouble, and he brought them out of their distress. He stilled the storm to a whisper;
the waves of the sea were hushed. They were glad when it grew calm,
and he guided them to their desired haven.
—Psalm 107:28-30

Chapter 19

My Dirty Little Secret

Being busy does not always mean real work. The object of all work is production or accomplishment and to either of these ends there must be forethought, system, planning, intelligence, and honest purpose, as well as perspiration. Seeming to do is not doing.
—Thomas Edison

I like to think I'm a normal girl. I fly by the seat of my pants and live life on the edge. I've got friends; I go out on the weekends, and by most standards remain social. I do, however, possess a secret. A dirty deed I try to keep under wraps for fear that if it got out, I'd single-handedly destroy all my appearances. I, Heather Thompson Day, was a Facebook stalker.

I was introduced to Facebook by one of my best friends, who decided to set me up an account equipped with a few cyber friends I could call my own. I had no idea that this small maneuver would propel me into an abyss of insanity.

When I first started, I was new to the game. I had zero tagged pictures, and I hardly remembered my password enough to check for messages. I don't remember exactly when the switch occurred. It seemed to have taken place slowly over time, a day-by-day process that has left me a mere shell of my former self.

If you were to look at my Facebook a year or so in, you would've had a direct peek into the window of my soul. From my frequently updated statuses to my pictures, my Facebook had taken on a life of its own. Oftentimes I found myself returning home from an evening with friends, rushing to check for comments with one sleeve of my coat still on. Suddenly I found myself taking pictures only because I wanted to post them online. My virtual world was colliding with my real one, and it was starting to get ugly.

The problem is that I don't think I'm alone in this. I have seen Myspace solitarily destroy friendships and leave no prisoners, as arguments ensue over the prestigious "Top Friend Ranking." I have seen once happily together couples fall to shambles in the clutches of "private messaging." (Note here: If it needs to be said in a private message, something sultry is going on.) My point is, just as quickly as this once-plentiful recreational arena can bring you joy, it can switch to a tawdry scene of cyber flirting and online bullying, wreaking havoc and leaving trails of complete devastation in its path, all from the click of the mouse.

Facebook is not the arch nemesis. It has its accomplices to get the job done, such as Myspace (which I've been sober of for almost three years now), Twitter, and High Five. All other stealthily crafted Internet communities created to distract their operator for hours at a time to do, well, "virtually" nothing. After calculating all my time lost through Facebook and other cyber networks, I came to the conclusion that I could have been working on a master's or doctoral thesis with my now-lost hours. After realizing that if I'd spent half of the time I spent on Facebook on something productive and relevant to my future, such as God or school, I would've been well on my way to a future nothing short of euphoria. This conclusion left me with no other alternative but to shut my Facebook down.

It had taken on a life of its own, and I needed to find myself again. I am being sarcastic, but only a little. I seriously think social networking sites have drastically affected our generation. The purpose of this rant is to speak out and show other wayward cyber souls that you are not alone. We shall overcome. If shutting down your site seems like too much of an extreme, at least try to start looking at the clock and timing how much of your day is actually spent in this virtual reality.

The truth is, those people aren't even your friends. I came to grips with this reality after I was sick for about two whole days. In two whole days I got approximately three phone calls. (Excluding my mother and boyfriend, who blew up my mobile like I have free minutes.) The entire time that my phone was in the dead zone, I was a celebrity on Facebook, and I had the picture comments to prove it! I received messages in the virtual world, but in the real world, nothing.

It's time to turn a new leaf, my fellow cyber geeks. Let's go outside and make "real friends." For once, enjoy the serenity of snapping photos with your comrades without being harassed for the next six hours about when you're going to *finally* upload them. Quit reading the wall to walls of you and your secret crush, and get out there and flirt. (Reminder: "Poking" does not constitute actual flirting.) There has been a breakdown in society, my friends, and we need to evoke change!

How has social networking affected this generation? you ask. Well, for starters, it seems that no one is really all that interested in growing up anymore, and I blame Facebook. Hear me out here. Everyone is more concerned with looking cool than actually being productive. I can't tell you how many friends, 22 years of age and up, I have seen posting statuses about how drunk they got the night before. I desperately want to comment, "Cool, did you buy it yourself? Did you go up to the salesclerk, pass them your REAL driver's license, and purchase actual booze?" Some of you are 30 years old. Get a life.

Does getting drunk constitute an alert? Cool, you drink. Notify me when you do something that is actually noteworthy, such as when you get a job, buy a house, and finish school, whatever. Alcohol is glorified: if you drink it you will instantly become cool. It's pathetic. I also detest how those who don't drink are somehow "uncool." People don't really know how to act around you anymore. It's as though they are hanging out with their pious grandmother and they don't have much to connect with you on. If alcohol is the only way you know how to have a good time, I think that says a lot about your personality, or lack thereof.

While we are on the subject, have you noticed how extremely narcissistic social media makes otherwise perfectly great people? If you can scroll through 100 posted photos and not find one of you with even one other person, something is definitely wrong. I don't know how many more pictures of a girl making a kissy face in the mirror I can see before I throw up. Many girls post pictures of themselves in their bikini in the dead of winter standing in their living room. If there is no sand, there should be no bathing suit! I also like how an ordinary person can say "Today's my birthday!" and receive five "likes" and comments. A random hot person can say "So sleepy," and they get 60. What universe has this stuff propelled us in? It is sucking up all our time, but is it actually doing us any good?

I realize now that Satan doesn't need us to be doing something necessarily bad in order to keep us from fulfilling our destiny. He just needs us to be doing something, anything, that keeps us busy. As long as we are too busy to dig deep and try to figure out what exactly God placed us on this earth to do, Satan wins. That's it.

That's what he doesn't want you to know. You were put on this earth for a mission, and anything, as harmless as it may be, that may distract you from fulfilling that mission is something that Satan wants to make sure you keep around. He wants you busy. He doesn't care what it's with; he just wants it to be anything different than what you're supposed to be doing. So don't give him the opportunity to distract you. Take a good, hard look at who you are and where you want to be, and spend your time doing things that are going to get you there. He has a plan for you. What is your plan for yourself?

> *"For I know the plans I have for you," declares the Lord,*
> *"plans to prosper you and not to harm you,*
> *plans to give you hope and a future."*
> —*Jeremiah 29:11*

Chapter 20

Mistakes Do Not Define Christianity—Love Does

*The art of acceptance is the art of making someone who has just done
you a small favor wish that he might have done you a greater one.*
—Martin Luther King, Jr.

I was in my church pew one weekend, and before the hymns and before the choir sang, I noticed this darling, tiny Asian child that sat in front of me. When I first sat down, she turned and smiled at me. Her dark hair was dangling from her loosely knitted bun, and her grin revealed one missing tooth that caused me to open my eyes and stick my tongue out at her playfully. She hushed her laughter and raised her hands in amusement at me as a sign for me to touch them. I did. We continued our facial games back and forth from time to time throughout the service, and when I kneeled down to pray, I felt her climb beneath her pew and touch my knees.

At some point during the sermon her mother handed her a chocolate bar to keep her occupied. She ate it, smiling at me the whole way, and licked the wrapper as she went along. I began to laugh as I saw the mess she had created; her fingers were covered in a thick, dark, gooey substance as the chocolate melted all over her hands and mouth. The mess did not deter her, and she continued to lick her fingers and her chin as she enjoyed each bite. Before she popped the last bite into her mouth, she looked at me and held the candy up as if to offer me a piece of her treasure. I declined, and she wasted no time devouring the last morsels.

My eyes went back to the preacher; then all of a sudden it happened. The same child I had been making faces with, playing patty-cake with, and sticking my tongue out at, the same beautiful little girl with the same messed-up bun and chubby cheeks, leaned forward to touch me, and I winced. I shot back into my pew, and my face reeked of pure horror as I saw her filthy little chocolate-stained hands reaching out to touch me. I lost my breath at the thought of those hands touching my expensive outfit and freshly cleaned skin. I flinched, not because she had changed—she had the same smile and same chubby cheeks that had first won my heart—but because now she was dirty.

I tell you this story because, much like the little girl in the pew in front of me, in life you will always meet different types of people. They will come at different walks on your journey and will represent different things at different times. Some will be beautiful and fun and will make you want to do nothing but throw your arms around them and seep as much of their soul into yours as possible before they are gone. And then all of a sudden, you'll watch them do something foolish that is superficial and of no real consequence to them as people. But you'll see them blemished now and look at those same hands you once held, and all you'll see is dirty, stained fingers.

Embrace these people, because to someone you will, one day, be that person. One day someone will see you soiled, and flinch. You will reach out to the same person who once understood you, and you will see them step back in anguish, perhaps even disgust. Not because you've changed, not because you're now different, but because, at that moment, all they can see is the residue of all your mistakes. That's what happens when we take people at face value. Our eyes aren't trained to see past the muck to the beautiful hands that are beneath them. Our eyes are trained only to see filth, and so we flinch.

We forget that chocolate and dirt, much like regret and shame, can be washed. I know this, because I wouldn't stand a chance in the presence of God if this were not true. Yes, the soot can be washed away, so much so that anyone who came after would never even believe it was ever there, but the look on your face when they show you their dirt simply can't. Your rejection will be embedded into their skin like an earring into freshly pierced flesh. It will stay with them; with you.

Sadly but often that facial expression, our first initial reaction to so quickly condemn someone else, can be the deciding factor in whether or not they make an effort to get clean. If I am dressed up and slip in the mud, I will certainly shower so as not to infect the rest of my clothes with my dirty hands. I will make an effort not to touch my face or pat my dress, because I can see that a part of me is unclean, while the rest of me is spotless. When I see my white dress, tamely hair, and powdered face, I'll hold my hands in the air until I am able to get to running water and pat them dry.

The opposite is true, however, if I am already dirty. If I'm already filthy and slip in the mud, I'll wipe my hands on that same dress because it is ruined anyway. I'll wipe the sweat from my eyes, brush back my hair, and rub my hands together, because I am already tainted.

I still feel bad about flinching from that tiny girl; her shoulders shrank as she turned away from me, and she didn't give me as much as a glance for the rest of the service. I lost my friend that afternoon, when it would have been so much easier just to open my purse and hand her a tissue.

I remembered this experience years later when walking my nephew into church. I was wearing a brand-new white dress that I had been told looked ravishing on me. I loved it, and I was excited to wear it out again. I was walking with my nephew, and it was summer and he was wearing shorts. We were doing the whole "one, two, three" number, where "three" signifies that the child should jump in the air, and you on one side and someone else on the other can lift them up and swing them in the air. My nephew Caiden has done "one, two, three" many times before. This wasn't his first rodeo, and yet somehow he forgot to lift his legs, and so they just kind of dragged on the ground. He skinned his knee pretty badly, and when he looked down, all he saw was blood.

Once he saw the blood, he started to cry and turned to me for help. My first thought was *Oh no, my white dress*, but my next thought was of that beautiful, tiny, little girl with the chocolate on her fingers in that church pew. Without a second thought I picked him up and let him cradle himself into my arms and body. His tears slipped down my chest, and his snot rubbed on my shoulders.

"It's OK," I whispered. "You'll be OK." And eventually his sobs calmed down and he melted there in my arms. When I was able to set him back down, I saw that blood had gotten all over my pretty white dress. I could have been upset, but I wasn't. This time I had done things the right way. I smiled at my reflection, and was glad that this time when a child reached for me I didn't push them away for fear of getting dirty.

Sex, alcohol, and drugs are all things our church does not condone, yet some of its members have done them. If someone reaches out to us in embarrassment, who are we to give them scorn? If you ask me, these sins, while bad, and the sins we commit against ourselves, though still heavy, are not as strong as the bat we swing against each other. When we hurt someone else, start a rumor, call them names, and look at them in disgust, that sin will change them. That sin is unbearable because it not only rejects love, but also may cause them to reject themselves. They may start to think that if they are already dirty, there's no point in trying to keep it contained—they're already ruined. No one is ever ruined. So please, if someone ever reaches out to touch you, ignore their smudges. Right then, all they need is a napkin.

The Lord does not look at the things people look at.
People look at the outward appearance,
but the Lord looks at the heart.
—1 Samuel 16:7

Chapter 21

Your Obituary

While I thought that I was learning how to live,
I have been learning how to die
—Leonardo Da Vinci

I wrote my own obituary once. I think it was a project for school or something. When the idea was thrown at me, I immediately thought it was ridiculous. I'm not dead. I don't really want to pretend to be dead or make up the scenario of why I had died. I even had to interview a few people in my family to see what they would say about me after I was gone. It was for a writing class. No spiritual lesson behind it. I was mistaken, though. Everything in life has the potential to teach us something spiritually— everything. This is what I wrote:

"Heather Marie Thompson was born January 1, 1987, in Berrien Springs, Michigan. Heather was the youngest of her four siblings, and was born to Joel and Vicki Thompson. Heather died in a tragic car accident that has devastated her friends and family. She was only 23 years old. Heather was a graduate of Andrews University, and was still in attendance while she pursued her graduate studies. She double-majored and received her B.A. in journalism and communication, and was studying for an M.A. in interdisciplinary communications. Her goal was to become a professor of communications/creative writing and teach the gift of the written word at Christian universities. Heather had published one book, *Hook, Line, and Sinker: A Practical Guide to Dating and Relating*, and was in the process of finishing her second piece, *Cracked Glasses*, a devotional for young adults.

"Heather was described by her mother as 'passionate.' She also said that Heather 'loved to write.' 'Heather started writing when she was able to hold a pen. She always said she found peace there and felt that that was her gift from God and that she was going to be held accountable for how she used it.'

"Her father added, 'Heather was extremely high-energy, and extremely creative. As soon as she would finish one project she'd start another.'

"Heather's untimely death did leave many of her writing projects unfinished. Her sister said that she would 'want to be remembered as a girl who lived up to her dreams for herself, and who was crazy about Christ.'

"A celebration service for Heather's life will be held at Pioneer Memorial church, the church where Heather was a member. Heather believed that reading God's Scripture was pertinent to salvation. Her favorite Bible verse was 'I have hidden your word in my heart that I might not sin against you' (Psalm 119:11)."

After I wrote that, I realized that if I had died that day, I would have had more things unfinished than finished. I thought about my mission, and about how often I get so distracted with just the routine of life that I end up doing nothing. I wondered about what people would have really said about me had I not been the one doing the interviews. I wondered how people besides my family would remember me, and whether or not I had really ever done anything that would make me memorable.

Sure, I had finished a book, but I'm also a writer. I should be writing. What have I done that was unexpected? What change had I initiated in which I surprised even myself? What legacy had I left behind?

I am almost obsessed with this desire to have my life be worth something. I want to make God proud. I want Him to look at me in heaven and say, "Well done, my good and faithful servant."

I have countless conversations with Christ throughout my day. I ask Him all the time to use me. I've even found myself saying, "I know I may not be much, but use me anyway." Or "I know there are better, more deserving candidates, others who seem to have this uncanny ability to make whatever they touch turn to gold. I know that I am probably not first or second or even third on Your list of people to use, but please, use me anyway."

I mean that. God first went to someone else with His visions and prophetic message for the Adventist Church and they turned Him down, and so then He picked Ellen White. I don't care if I am not God's first pick for a really delicate yet important issue; I just want Him to use me anyway.

How much sooner would Christ come back if to be sincerely used by God were the prayer on all of our hearts? It is my belief that the Adventist Church is the last-day church. I believe that if we ever get this thing together—this message of hope, of the Sabbath, of the Second Advent—if we ever figure out how not just to preach overseas, but to get involved right here at home, God will return in the blink of an eye. I firmly believe that.

I believe He has a message and is refusing to come back to take us home until all have heard it. I believe He is waiting for a few more precious souls that He knows would be ablaze if someone would just reach them. I believe He is waiting on you, and me, to finish His work. You may not be beautiful. You may not have a way with words or have any significant talents or any notable qualities that make people pick you out in a room. But guess what, God can use you anyway. We have no excuses.

If I can encourage you to do any strange task that might actually take an hour or so of your effort, I encourage you to write your own obituary. Think about what it would say if you really died today, and about what things you would leave unfinished. The great thing for us is that, as of yet, we're still here. There is still time to stay the course. You see, our obituaries aren't written yet. Our story is still unfolding, and the last page is still blank. So until your pen runs out of ink, keep writing.

My flesh and my heart may fail,
but God is the strength of my heart and my portion forever.
—Psalm 73:26

Chapter 22

Picking My Poison

Hypocrisy is not generally a social sin, but a virtue.
—Judith Martin

A couple years ago I had a very diplomatic conversation with some secular friends of mine about sex before marriage. I told them it was wrong. I passionately recited to them the verse about your body being a temple. I looked them in the eyes and told them that if they had sex before marriage, then one day, after truly falling in love and getting married, they were going to wish that their spouse had been their first everything. They were going to wish that they had been able to give them something special and untainted. They would wish that they could have shared with them a piece of themselves that no other person in the entire world had experienced with them before that moment. I told them that if they had sex before marriage, one day they'd regret it.

I told them that because I believed it. I was quite the advocate of true intimacy after hearing a series on purity that touched me. After I finished my speech and we went out for the evening, I felt good about the way I had argued my case. I still felt good as I entered the party, and even better as I asked the guy running the keg to fill up my beer. You see, I had it right, and that made me feel good. I wasn't sleeping with anyone. A few beers and rum and cokes later I was still right, and still abstinent. In fact, I was a lot of things, one of which was a hypocrite.

Just because sex wasn't my problem at that moment didn't make me pure. In fact, I was far from it. I think that's one of Satan's war tactics, getting us so caught up in what we are doing right that we never try to fix what we are still doing wrong. So instead we put ourselves on these pedestals of self-righteousness without ever realizing that we have just picked our poison.

Now, I am obviously not saying that we shouldn't point out one sin from another. I am simply saying that it is wrong to lecture someone else without then turning the microscope on to ourselves. I was convicted of one thing because of an excellently laid-out speaking series on purity, but since no one mentioned alcohol that day specifically, I continued on in my own hypocrisy. Perhaps I was the reason 60 percent of young people are leaving the church. They had a conversation with me and watched me living in sin, all the while professing Christianity. You see where this can cause confusion.

Hypocrites, especially those laced in Christian clothing, are one of my biggest pet peeves. I say that knowing full well that oftentimes I am one of them. Of course, realizing that there is a problem is a good thing. I share these things with you about myself because I know I am not alone. My father has said to me on more than one occasion after reading things I write, "Can't you stick to fiction? Quit telling everyone your business." But I promised God a long time ago that if He would bless me, I would write down the things I have learned while on this pursuit of salvation, and that I would do so candidly. There is strength in numbers. At times I've been the biggest loser ever, and guess what, God has used me anyway. If you hand yourself over in spite of what you've done, God will use you anyway.

I've noticed in my life that there are a lot of people who are quick to condemn other people without first checking for their name in the sand. I've heard people go on and on about how they don't drink and how they don't party; meanwhile they're on their way with their boyfriend/girlfriends to fill their birth-control prescription, or vice versa. What's the difference? If we are really the generation who is going to incite revival, I think we first have to be revived.

We're quick to quote verses from the Bible that make us look good, and just as quick to close the Bible before our eyes hit anything that exposes us to ourselves. You can put up a front for pretty much everyone, but tricking yourself is difficult, and fooling God is impossible. We have to start modeling genuine, authentic Christianity for our secular peers and uphold one another. If you don't understand why others aren't rushing to follow you, maybe it's because you aren't living all that different from how they are.

If you feel convicted to point out someone else's flaws, do it, but do it in love, and be ready to take a nice hard look at yourself in the mirror afterward and make sure everything you were prescribing is in your own medicine cabinet. A lot of us think being a Christian means we ourselves are the judges of humanity. And so we go around making sure to tear each other down, forgetting that God's mission to earth wasn't to hold us captive by our pasts, but to point us forward toward the future. If we want to mimic Christ, let's tap in to His ever-powerful message of love.

You see, in my case it was partying that made me a hypocrite. I can't speak for you; only you can know your shortcomings. I do know, though, that you can take it from me: Preaching abstinence with one side of your mouth and taking a shot from the other doesn't make you a Christian. It doesn't make you right, it doesn't make God proud, and it doesn't make you pure. The only thing it does do is make you another bad example. It gives every questioning soul out there seeking truth a pretty good reason to stay clear of "Christianity."

One of the most important answers I have had to dig deep into my soul to find is to the question "How do I change?" I want to be that person that God wants me to be. I want to be the child my parents thought they were raising. I want to be that friend, that teacher, that mother, that wife, that I read about in inspiring novels and see in motivational movies. I want to be authentic, but how do I start?

Here's the truth. Want to know how you change? You develop an intimate relationship with Jesus Christ. That's it. That's the golden ticket. You develop a deep, loving, passionate relationship with your Lord, and then you let Him change you. It is impossible to surround yourself with His goodness and not be changed. Develop that bond, and then watch as who you are becomes washed away.

The good news is that there is hope. We are the makers of our own destiny. My sister once told me that a professor of hers said a statement to her class that rocked her profoundly. He told them, "If you don't change the direction that you're going, you may end up there." The question I had to ask myself was "Where exactly am I headed?" Do you know where you're going?

If I speak in the tongues of men or of angels, but do not have love,
I am only a resounding gong or a clanging cymbal.
—1 Corinthians 13:1

Chapter 23

Old, Raggedy Sneakers

People are pretty much alike. It's only that our differences are more susceptible to definition than our similarities.
—Linda Ellerbee

The simplicity of children floors me. Their ability to resolve the largest of issues with such precision and grace is something, as adults, we far too often overlook. I went to a seminar on Andrews University's campus yesterday put on by a friend of mine, Pierre Quinn, and he opened it by asking the audience to do something that they probably hadn't done since elementary school. He asked us to imagine. I loved that, because somewhere in between learning how to color inside the lines and puberty, we lose the most precious gift ever bestowed on the human mind: imagination.

I've mentioned to many people that my family is the pinnacle of racial equality. As a completely interracial family, we are so deeply intertwined that I am quick to forget that the rest of the world isn't. Even in the particular town where I have lived most of my life, the community was shielded in a way. It's like a mini-New York City. There are so many different people from so many different backgrounds. Your neighbors could look just like you or be from a country you've never even heard of. It's easy to forget that outside of the multicultural radius where I grew up, there are still people who just don't get it.

We are living in an ever-changing world. Society is evolving right before our very eyes. We're technologically superior, medically complex, and philosophically advanced. In the past 100 years we have learned to fly, invented the telephone, even created an instrument that can connect millions of people globally called the Internet. This, right here, right now, is the American dream.

When it comes to each other, however, we are still mediocre. We still pass each other by, unconcerned with the story behind the person.

I myself love stories. I love sitting down and thinking about my life in tiny sections and pieces and honing in on those moments that seemed inconsequential to me at the time, but that I know I can write about and gain some sort of spiritual application. The best part about stories is that we all have them. They are a part of us, and those stories all strung together are what make us who we are. Stories are vital, and yet we rarely ask people what theirs is.

Instead, we just pass one another. I find it funny that we need no reason to hate someone. We hate because they are too thin, too fat, too Black, too White, too rich, and too poor. We hate on a whim, but we need a really good reason to love. By doing that, we miss out on the greatest gift of humanity—brotherhood/sisterhood—with no reason.

My brother has two radiantly handsome sons, and I am not just saying that because we share a bloodline. These boys are precious. Though they are brothers, they share one unique physical difference. You see, Jeziah is Black, and Jaylen is biracial, but by all outward appearance White.

My brother told me a story a couple years ago that happened when he picked the boys up from school. It was a moment that we knew would occur at some point; it was inevitable. We knew that sooner or later someone would question their relationship because of their outside appearance. Jeziah's friends told him they didn't believe Jaylen was his brother, because he was "White."

It had happened to me as a child. My mother is White and I am Brown, and from childhood to adulthood it's seemed to be a perplexing conundrum for people to understand that White and Black people are capable of reproducing together. (Even though, in my opinion, my mother and I look very much alike.) So it wasn't the situation that perplexed me. I had already experienced it and knew it was only a matter of time before they would also. The situation was typical. It was their response to the circumstances that left me reeling.

A group of boys formed around my nephew as Jalyen and his mother went to meet Jeziah and lead him to the car.

"There's no way that's your brother," one of the kids said assuredly. "You guys aren't even the same color."

Now, my nephews are very close. For years my brother even dressed them in matching outfits. They are also pretty similar in age, and so the bond they have formed is intense. Naturally, Jeziah began to get agitated with his buddies from school when they insisted that his little brother didn't belong to him.

"He is so my brother!" he shouted at the mob of boys that was rallying against him in disbelief. They continued to disagree for a moment, and instead of jumping in, my brother stepped back to see exactly how this would play out without his interference. Exasperated, Jeziah pointed to his shoes and told the boys to look.

You see, I get on my nephews a lot because they are obsessed with superheroes. I've been explaining to them that they need to broaden their horizons and make sure that they have more to talk about in conversations with people than just comic books. This day, however, it was their love for Batman that helped them.

"We are brothers! See," my nephew told his friends, "we both have matching Batman sneakers!"

The mood of the boys circling around my nephews quickly changed from perplexity to acknowledgment as they said, "Oh, OK," and then ran for their bus.

When my brother told me that story, I was reminded again of the beauty, simplicity, and imagination of children. I marveled at their ability to communicate without the interference of adults who "know everything."

I wish superhero sneakers could solve more problems. I hope the next time I go to dismiss someone because my high horse says they are nothing like me, I see the simple familiarity of a rising chest, a beating heart, and a pair of eyes. I hope the next time I am brazen enough to assume someone else has nothing to teach me, I recognize that they have a story to tell, much as I do.

One thing I love about teaching interpersonal communications is that at the end of the year the students are supposed to produce a portfolio explaining how the various concepts apply to their lives. I love the portfolios, because I see how these students that I have been getting to know for the past three to four months have their own story that I knew nothing about. You may think you know someone, but I am learning that there is so much depth hidden beneath the face that you may casually say hello to. You need to enter these lives with a certain air of delicateness. You have no idea what they've seen, and you never can assume. One portfolio shared 15 years of sexual abuse at the hands of a stepfather. Others shared time spent in prison, the murder of a mother, rape, and the deterioration of important relationships. These students, that I thought I knew, were going through some heavy stuff, and had I not read their portfolios, I would never have known. People are precious; take time to hear their stories.

We spend so much time trying to explain our differences with one another through larger-than-life speakers and racial equality gatherings. Adults need government initiatives and educational programs, along with scientific research, to prove that we are all made up of the same stuff. Perhaps if we looked at the similarities we share more often, we'd see that the brotherhood of humanity isn't as distant as it seems.

Black or White, fat or thin, rich or poor, we all share some piece of common ground, whether it is simple or complex. Children don't need much to realize that we aren't so different. I'm sure we too can draw parallels with those people who to us seem so different. As long as we are all Bible-fearing Christians, we can agree that our genealogy all traces back to one couple. If we can agree on nothing else, at least we can agree on that. That, and the fact that I'm sure all of us have at least one pair of old, raggedy sneakers.

There is neither Jew nor Greek,
neither slave nor free,
nor is there male and female,
for you are all one in Christ Jesus.
—Galatians 3:28

Chapter 24

Put Up or Shut Up

*A lot of people run a race to see who is fastest. I run to see who has
the most guts, who can punish himself into exhausting pace,
and then at the end, punish himself even more.*
—Steve Prefontaine

My freshman year of college I attended a school in Indiana. I was there on a track scholarship and had, by all of my preconceived notions, "made it." Track was my life, and in many forms is still one of my fondest memories and deepest regrets. I dedicated six years of my life to it, and later transferred to a school without a track program and perhaps lost a tiny piece of who I was, though I gained a much greater sense of who I would become.

At the end of my freshman year I had qualified for Christian Nationals in the women's 4x400-meter relay. If you're unfamiliar with track and field, the 4x400-meter relay has four athletes who each run one lap around the track and then pass the baton to the next teammate. I was nervous, injured, and had a pretty good idea that I would be transferring to a new school in the fall, making this the last race of my life.

I wanted to end on a high. I had suffered my fair share of losses that year. Running track in college was nothing like running track in high school. In high school I was a big fish in a small pond. I rarely lost. Out of my four years there, I qualified for state twice. I don't think I ever placed high while at state, but I was happy with just going there. It was the only time in high school that you stayed the night in a hotel with your sports team. We went to dinner at a swanky restaurant, and as long as I qualified to run at the state meet, I considered my season a success.

In college, however, I was actually physically afraid to go to track practice. It wasn't a joke, and there were many afternoons that I would take a break, only to vomit before hearing my coach scream my name to get back to work. I kind of goofed off a bit in high school. I could eat a stack of nachos and then take my place on the track, and still win. In college everything I did was highly monitored. On meet days I was confined to bananas and peanut butter. I wasn't running for fun anymore; I was being trained to win.

I lost a lot in college. I was sometimes fast enough to make it to the faster heat, but never fast enough to win the whole race. I honestly don't think I won one race on my own my whole year in both indoor and outdoor collegiate track season. Everyone else told me that freshman year was the hardest, that learning to lose was a tough lesson, but that the next year I'd see my fair share of wins again. Well, I knew I probably wouldn't come back the next year. I loved my track team, but I just didn't really feel as though being at that school at that time in my life was where God wanted me. I had no idea where He did want me, but something just told me it wasn't where I was.

When the gun sounded, the first leg of our relay took off and got us a pretty good start. Even now as I write, I can feel my heart begin to skip a beat as my mind takes me back. When it was my turn, I felt the baton push into my hand, and I took off. I sprinted as fast as I could for the first 60 meters, which was my plan, and then pulled back. I pulled back because the 400 is one of the hardest races to run, and I was extremely nervous about running out of steam and dying out on the last straightaway of the track. I pulled back and let people pass me.

I pulled back because the very first race I ran in my college outdoor season was a 400-meter dash, and I completely died out on the last straightaway. I sprinted that thing as fast as I could because I wanted to impress everyone. I wanted my coaches to see that their money toward my education was a smart investment. I cannot even describe to you the feeling my body went through on that last straightaway. It literally was like my legs turned to Jell-O and a gorilla jumped on my back. I was probably going slower than if I had walked myself to the finish line. I was simply gassed out, and I couldn't let that happen again, especially at nationals.

I paced myself on the first straightaway and waited for that last 150 meters, where I would sprint into the finish line. My eyes hit my mark halfway through my last curve, and I took off as hard and powerful as possible. I felt the wind bite my face as I started gaining back the ground I had lost. The last few meters came, and I handed the baton to the finishing leg, and then I sat down and cried.

I cried because I didn't fall to my knees at the end, I didn't collapse, I didn't even feel that weak. I cried because I had saved too much. It was the last race I would ever run, and I didn't leave everything I had on that track. I cried because, in that moment, I knew that "better safe than sorry" was for losers.

To this day, that race makes me shudder. It stings my pride worse than the time I got disqualified at my state track meet in high school, worse than the time I tripped over my shoelace in eighth grade and got that scar on my right knee, worse than that first outdoor college meet when I needed to show my coaches what I was made of and pushed my body so hard that I died out and threw up on the finish line, and still got last place. You see, this one takes the cake, not because we were defeated (I had been beat before), but because this time I had defeated myself.

The reason I tell this story isn't to bask in my glory days, or even to instill some lifelong lesson of tenacity. I tell this story to show you my biggest fear in life: playing it "too safe" when it comes to God's mission for me.

At the end of this world I want to look back and know I left it all on the track. I want to be exhausted, I want to be empty, I want to collapse in His arms one day and know that I left no rock unturned. I'm challenging you to save nothing. Don't hold back anything when it comes to your loved ones and Him. They may have their gates, but you may be their drawbridge. If you have your devotionals every morning and your vespers every evening, even better! Just make sure you are always giving away just as much of Him as you are taking in.

I want to share with you a Bible verse that has been helpful to me in this race called life that I am running. You see, like it or not, this is the last leg of earth's journey. This is not just a message that I have put together for any people at any time—I put together this message specifically for Christ's most effective, most passionate, most capable arsenal that He has in this war that's going on for salvation. I put this message together for you! Christ's generation of young people that He has raised up for such a time as this. He has brought you into existence for this exact moment to do something incredible: finish the last leg of this race.

The verse I'd like you to hold on to is Isaiah 40:31: "But those who hope in the Lord will renew their strength. They will soar on wings like eagles; they will run and not grow weary, they will walk and not be faint."

What a promise! This isn't track, and if you give it all you got you can go for more than 300 meters! If you push yourself, guess what, you will run and not grow weary! You will walk and not be faint! I'll leave you with this thought. Sometimes the closest to God someone else is going to get is you. And I can tell you one thing: Jesus was still preaching at His own crucifixion. My God saves nothing.

> *Whatever you do, work at it with all your heart,*
> *as working for the Lord, not for human masters.*
> *— Colossians 3:23*

Chapter 25

Smelly Kelly

We need to find God, and he cannot be found in noise and restlessness.
God is the friend of silence. See how nature—trees, flowers, grass—grows in
silence; see the stars, the moon and the sun, how they move in silence. . . .
We need silence to be able to touch souls.
—Mother Teresa

I believe in the power of silence. It's not natural for me to be silent; I myself am riddled with opinions and love words. Words are how I express myself, and writing them down allows me to figure out who I am. Regardless, I have learned throughout my life the blessings of silence, and that sometimes silence can be deafening.

I'm not sure exactly when it was that I met Smelly Kelly. I went to a tiny school in a tiny town, and it seemed to me that she had just always been there. Her birth name was of course not Smelly Kelly, just Kelly, and the students added the Smelly part at some point in junior high. It was the age of growth and changes, and Kelly had obviously not yet used deodorant. This would all probably be fine if we didn't all have to go to gym class. Kelly learned to despise gym.

Kids used to laugh and point at her. Sometimes they'd whisper, and other times they'd chant as she walked by. I never participated, or even wanted to. I didn't hate her, feel disgust toward her, or even think she was all that smelly; I just simply didn't care one way or the other. Though I was not part of the attacks, my silence, I'm sure, spoke volumes. It told Kelly, and everyone else who saw me mute, that I was no better than the chorus leader. I was just as guilty and just as wicked.

I'm not sure if I worried that had I said something the mob, which really wasn't a mob at all, would turn on me, or if I was just that insensitive—that watching her tears meant nothing to me. One thing I am sure of is I was a witness to this abuse for almost a year before I realized what we had done.

I went into the bathroom one day before gym class and found Kelly balled up on the floor like a scared rat before a scientist. She was holding her knees with her arms. The water was running, and soap was in the sink.

Her eyes were crying, but her voice was not. Her voice was howling like a dog rejected from its pack. She was wearing a pair of faded blue jeans and a once-white T-shirt that was now a distant brown. She had her hair tied up into one long braid, and the light shone down on her in such a way that the beads of sweat on her collarbone became visible.

Within the two seconds it had taken for me to get close enough for her to see me, I had already contemplated whether I would keep walking or acknowledge her sight. I had told myself that it would probably be embarrassing for her and that I should pretend not to see her and continue on my way. Besides, the bell would ring soon, and if I did not keep on track I might receive a tardy. I told myself that, but seemed to forget to send the memo to my legs, because before I knew it, I was beside her, asking what was wrong.

I've been on the outside before. There was an "I hate Heather club" at my elementary school. I learned a lot from the outside. I learned that children can be cruel, and that I never could pick up arithmetic, but mean behavior was something I could be taught. I had kids who hated me, and just as many who wanted to be me, and so it created a tough environment. I got really used to feeling alone in the midst of a crowd, and I still think that may have been God preparing me for my future. Perhaps one day there will again be an "I hate Heather club," except this time I will have learned how to feel comfortable in my own skin. I knew what it felt like to live on the outside, and so though I didn't speak up for Kelly, I never wanted her to feel alone.

"It's true," she said without looking at me. "I am smelly."

It was funny, because in that instant, with the dim light holding her face and neck tightly, I realized that Kelly was actually pretty. Beneath her nappy hair and ugly clothes was a pair of high cheekbones and deep-set almond eyes. Past the soot and smudges on her hands and under her nails were tiny, slender fingers and skin with the most beautiful complexion. As her eyes filled up with tears again, I saw her bite down on her perfectly pink lips and watched as her small-framed button nose began to flare its nostrils. Smelly Kelly was beautiful, and I wondered if anyone would ever know it.

I didn't know what to say to her. I realized then that she had come into the bathroom to wash under her arms with soap from the dispenser. My heart broke for her, and I instantly wanted to tell her how sorry I was that I had never stood up for her. I wanted to cry and beg for her forgiveness, to drag her out of that locker room and make a public statement to the rest of the class so that they too would see how wrong we all were. I didn't, though. I didn't say anything. I just placed my hand on top of hers and sat with her for 30 minutes in silence until the bell rang. When we got up to leave, she told me, "Thank you," and I told her that I didn't know what for.

I'm not sure where Kelly is now. We didn't form some lasting friendship from the situation, and I'm not sure now if we ever really mixed words again. I did see her at a fair a couple years ago. We both said hi and kept walking.

One summer I broke off my engagement two months before the wedding for various reasons. I wasn't speaking to anyone. I spent my days at work, and by the time I got home I was so exhausted from faking a smile that I would collapse into my pillow and cry until I had no tears left. My father came over one evening. I opened the door and then went right back to my bed.

"I don't want to talk," I told him, and put my face right back into my pillow.

"That's OK," he responded. "Neither do I."

He sat there with me in silence, neither of us speaking and neither of us wanting to. At some point, however, he lifted his hand and placed it on mine, and that's when I remembered sitting on that cold bathroom floor with Kelly. Suddenly I realized just exactly what she had thanked me for— the silence. The chance to do nothing but catch your breath and listen to your own heart beat.

I realized that in between who I was before and who I had grown to be, in between my lack of backbone then and tears now, in between that hello I shared with Kelly at the fair that really meant goodbye lay a calming in the silence; a power in the stillness that words could never have filled. Yes, silence has power. This I believe.

The one who has knowledge uses words with restraint,
and whoever has understanding is even-tempered.
Even fools are thought wise if they keep silent,
and discerning if they hold their tongues.
—Proverbs 17:27, 28

Chapter 26

Songs Need Words

The only guide to man is his conscience; the only shield to his memory is the rectitude and sincerity of his actions. It is very imprudent to walk through life without this shield, because we are so often mocked by the failure of our hopes and the upsetting of our calculations; but with this shield, however the fates may play, we march always in the ranks of honor.
— *Winston Churchill*

I always tell people, "If you can look at all your friends and notice that none of them is a Christian, then you need to reevaluate your Christianity."

I don't just say that to blow smoke or because I think it puts me on a high horse. I say it because it's true. I think that oftentimes, as Christians, we spend more of our efforts preaching to the choir than sculpting a message for the congregation. We pour our hearts into our sermons, sing from the soul, pray from the depths of our cores, sweat and pant and immerse ourselves in a message so profound and complex it could convert the worst of sinners. The only problem is they will never hear it as long as we are only sharing it among each other.

In third grade I was forced to be in choir. I say forced because, if I had had a choice, I would have probably stayed home. Don't get me wrong; I love singing. I sing by myself all the time. When I'm alone, I'm a regular Whitney Houston. I've been told, however, that there will be no platinum records in my future. I now know I'm not a singer, and if at any point I didn't know, my sisters told me. Nonetheless, there I was in choir, singing loudly.

One day my teacher had me stay after class. She was concerned for the upcoming concert because I was singing so loudly.

"I'm that bad?" I asked her. "I'm so bad that my voice is ruining the entire choir?"

I believed that this could be a possibility, but what does she expect? I was a kid. What did she want me to do? Pretend to sing and mouth "watermelon" the entire time? I just wanted to be a part of the group. My best friend in elementary school could sing like a canary. She was adorable and talented, and I just wanted to be like her.

"It's not that your voice is necessarily that bad," she answered me. "It's that you don't even know the words."

It was true. I often got so lost in trying to sound beautiful that I would "fa la la la la" over the verses. I was too busy riffing and holding high notes to worry about getting each and every word out correctly.

Recently I've had a sense that I'm running out of time—that if I don't get my life together, Hell pass me by. Have you ever felt that you know God has something good He wants to give you but you still haven't completely surrendered to Him and so things are kind of at a standoff?

I've been trying to look at my life from the outside. I've been analyzing my motives and have realized that though my heart's usually in the right place, my actions still aren't.

At one point I sifted through my social life and found that I didn't have one close friend who was a die-hard Christian. Most of my friends were agnostics, if not professed atheists. And those who were seeking God were still trying to make that connection between their behaviors and beliefs, much like I was. I can't help thinking that perhaps my circle of friends says even more about my Christianity. Maybe I purposely surrounded myself with those friends so that way I was always "the good one." Maybe that way I felt less guilty and less responsible. True Christianity is linked with balance.

I made sure to get balance out of my friendships. I now have the most inspiring friends. I attend the most inspiring Bible study on Friday evenings with a few of them. I have friends who want to shout on the mountaintops about this incredible Christ they've met, and they make me excited about the future of our generation. I have friends who, unlike me, did not grow up in spoon-fed Christian homes and yet are still crazy about Jesus Christ. I have friends that grew up in homes in which their parents didn't always provide them with a positive example of what it looks like to be an adult. I have friends who found God on their own, and when I listen to them speak with such passion and fervor about their relationships with God, it humbles me.

I may be the one with books, but I'm also the one with the perfect parents, the perfect example of marriage, and the perfect home. I'm the one with not much to moan about, and yet it took me till my 20s to really surrender my will to Christ. Isn't that unfortunate? I can't help wondering what things God could have used me for had I just connected with Him earlier.

Did you know that at the age of 18 you are in the prime of your existence physically? Somewhere between 18 and 21 we as humans stop growing. Somewhere between 18 and 21 we stop the growing process, and start the dying process. Our bodies literally, the second they are done growing, start dying. At 18 you are, figuratively and literally, in the prime of your life.

I often think, *If only I had surrendered my soul to Christ back when I was 16 or 17, or, better yet, 12. What ways could I have radically changed my circumstances just by serving Him?* It is too late for me to go back, but here's the exciting thing: Maybe it's not for you. Maybe you are in your prime, or maybe you are like me and have passed it. Either way, the bottom line is we have our whole lives before us, and I pray that you make a decision this week to use that life and your gifts to bring Him glory, and then just step back and watch what doors He opens.

You see, I can write some pretty stories. I can go to church and hold a Bible study. I can cry at worships and sing at song service. I can get an A in every religion class I've ever taken, date someone in the seminary, watch evangelical television, and always give tithe. I can do a lot of "right" things and still be incredibly wrong.

After all, anyone can sing at the top of their lungs. You can sing so loud everyone can hear you, so passionate everyone can see you, and so vibrant everyone can remember your name. But what's any of it really going to matter if all you are doing is singing a song without knowing any of the words?

Dear children, let us not love with words
or speech but with actions and in truth.
—1 John 3:18

Chapter 27

The Bus Stop

Live so that when your children think fairness, caring,
and integrity, they think of you.
—H. Jackson Brown, Jr.

When I was 6 years old, I was told I would be taking the bus to school. I was immediately aware that this was a terrible idea; my father, however, wasn't following my line of thinking. I didn't want to take the bus. I had never before been forced to ride the bus, and didn't see why I should have to now. I had, however, gotten glimpses of what the bus looked like from time to time, and it was scary. There were giant children on there, children that were hardly children at all. There were mean, unruly boys who I knew would pull my ponytail and call me names. Plus, there were weird kids, and who knew whom I would be forced to sit by?

I took extra time getting ready the morning my dad was supposed to walk me to the bus stop. I wore my peach culottes with a floral pattern and slid my white lacy socks on. I pulled my hair into a tightly knit bun and stared at my reflection in the mirror. My eyes welled up at the thought of what the coming moments would bring. I couldn't believe my dad was going through with this. Didn't he love me? I slipped on my sneakers and pinned the stray hairs from my bun into place.

I walked out of my bedroom and began to eat my breakfast; the realization of what was about to occur took full heat over my body, and I sobbed. I pleaded with and begged my father not to make me ride the bus. I made deals and promises I knew I'd never keep. I offered to do everyone's chores for a month, and he said we all needed to share the responsibility. I said he could deduct my allowance, which was only a couple dollars a week, and he said I should be saving. I said I'd get all A's, which he told me was expected. I said I'd do the laundry, dry the dishes, wash the car, and walk the dog, and he reminded me that I would be doing those things anyway, plus, we didn't own a dog.

It just wasn't making sense to me. We owned a car, so why should I be taking the bus? It suddenly hit me that maybe I had not played my cards right. Maybe he just didn't understand how much I did not want to get on that bus. I needed to up my game. I reached back into my mind and pulled out the next item on my arsenal.

I grabbed his arm and pulled my hair. I stomped my feet and let snot fall from my nose. I told him I'd do anything as long as he'd keep me off that bus. Regardless, there I was 10 minutes later, waiting at the bus stop. I watched the leaves roll past my untied sneakers and reached for my dad's hand. I had cajoled my father into at least walking me to the bus stop, even though it was right behind our apartment building. I squeezed his hand as if I were checking for his pulse as we stood there in silence. My father is a man of few words anyway. He answers most questions with the nod of his head and can somehow cram paragraphs into sentences.

I was a complete daddy's girl. I had spent years wedging myself into this man's soft spot, and I couldn't believe that he was turning on me now.

That's when I remembered crossing the street. You see, when I was growing up, I was not allowed to cross the street. My sister was allowed to, but she was also three years older than I was. I could cross the street only if my mom or dad was accompanying me. There were times that the kids at the complex across the street found toads, turtles, or other random critters that I wanted to see so desperately. My sister would cross the street, and then shout back to me all the details. I would stand at the end of my driveway, close my eyes, and take it all in. It was the closest I could get to actually being there.

My parents always told me that when I turned 6 I could cross the street by myself if I made sure to look both ways. I missed many toads and turtles that year, but finally the much-awaited day came. It was my sixth birthday, which just so happens to fall on New Year's Day. It was freezing out, but at midnight, and at my request, my parents agreed to walk me outside and let me cross the street by myself. It was a huge moment, and I still remember it. I looked both ways, and took those steps toward independence.

It was while remembering crossing the street that I realized the cold, hard truth about the bus. There was nothing I could do. I would be riding it.

I knew my dad like the back of my hand, and because of that, I also knew that if Father said I would be riding the bus that day, I would indeed be riding the bus. My dad always has follow-through. He never says something and then is coerced out of it. Once he says it, it's done. My arguments were arbitrary.

I felt the sweat collecting underneath my armpits as that yellow bus rolled around the corner. Tears welled up in my eyes again as I looked at my father one last time. I swallowed back the large lump that had collected in my throat and gave his wrist one last final squeeze, as if to signal to him that if there was ever a time to save me, it was now. He leaned down over me and kissed my forehead.

"This is going to be good for you," he whispered as the bus put on its brakes. "I'll be here when you get off to take you home."

I wanted him to change his mind. I wanted him to look in the windows and see all those children who were at least triple my size and realize they could kill me if they pleased. I wanted to be his baby girl right then; to morph back into early childhood and let him stick a pacifier in my mouth if it meant he would take me home. How well did we really know this driver? How sure were we that this bus was up to code? There seemed to be a lot of holes here, and I thought clarifying them would be nice before sticking me on a seat.

As he pulled his body upright, I clung to his neck. "I love you, Daddy!" I squealed in his ear, half sincere and half new war tactic. After all, I was desperate. I could feel my heart literally drop as I turned to walk onto the bus, admitting defeat. I wiped my tears as I found myself taking my place on the last seat of the bus. I pressed my face against the glass of the window. The chill of it bit my skin, and so I bit my lip and focused on my daddy. My father stood stationary, staring at me as the bus began to pull away. The air began to mist, and I kept my face pressed to the bus window as I found myself inching away from my father. He stood there, unflinching, like an old cypress oak in winter whose roots are firm and solid.

It may have been my imagination or the mist on the window, but I could swear that in that moment I saw my father cry. I couldn't be sure from the distance, but from where I was sitting I could have sworn I saw tears fill his eyes and his nostrils flare. I had never seen him cry before. Not when I fell off the handlebars of my bike and the smack on the concrete filled my mouth with blood, not when I stuck to my story about not stealing the quarters from his change jar, even though he knew I had. Not even when I wrote him a poem I was certain would bring him to his knees. But then, from the seat of the bus he had put me on, I saw it. I could barely recognize it. It was a look that was unfamiliar to me coming from him. I squinted as if that would give me a better view, but it was too late, and I lost him.

Sometimes I think that God is cruel. There have been times that I catch myself wondering how He can watch me down here, going through all this turmoil, and just stand still. I wonder why He won't just leap in and save me.

To this day, however, when I think of love, I think of my dad putting me on that bus. You see, there are always going to be buses filled with weird or mean people. There are always going to be bullies that pull your hair and call you names. There will always be situations that take you outside of your comfort zone, but you still have to get on the bus. It's the bus that makes you grow. It's surviving something you thought you could never get through that makes you strong.

I understand this now. And in those moments that I wonder where God is, I press my face to the glass of that bus window and I see, through the mist, that He is still there. With tears in His eyes He is rooting us through it. You can stomp your feet, pull your hair, cling to His neck, and beg for another way, but in truth, sometimes the hard path is the only path, and the easy road prepares you for nothing.

If you believe that Christ is returning and that you have work to do, that there is a devil who is never missing a moment to thwart you, you also have to believe in the power of the bus. There is transformation that takes place in suffering. And so love means not hiding you from tough times, but holding your hand as you get through them. You must be as nostalgic for the bad as you are for the good. And just like with my daddy, when the brakes push and the wind blows, when the ride is over and you get off stronger, Christ will be there, just as He promised, waiting to take you home.

Who shall separate us from the love of Christ?
Shall trouble or hardship or persecution or famine
or nakedness or danger or sword? . . .
No, in all these things we are more than conquerors
through him who loved us.
—Romans 8:35-37

Chapter 28

The Stage

All the world's a stage.
—*William Shakespeare*

In a small town, such as the one I am from, one thing becomes certain: Everyone knows everyone.

I went to dinner once with my best friend, who came home at the time to claim one of her American rights and vote. She's one of those extreme left-wing radicals who question whether or not September 11 wasn't actually some sort of conspiracy put on by the government to make us more concerned for our safety. I'd like to consider myself an Independent, though I often feel incredibly Republican when discussing much of anything with her.

Politics is such a touchy subject, and I am glad I have friends who keep me informed on the woes of both camps. I have a friend who is a staunch Republican and even goes so far as to say that he doesn't see how you can be Christian and vote Democrat. The fireworks really explode when these two opposing views are at the same table. They are both exceptionally bright and equally as adamant that their way is the right one.

At any rate, my best friend, whom I lovingly refer to as Posy-Rosy, and I went to dinner at a pizzeria in my town. It's one of those tiny hole-in-the-wall places right downtown that make you feel as if you're eating in your living room rather than paying a bill. While we were waiting, we discussed the events of the afternoon. In a journalism class I was taking I had put together a few pieces about the youth vote. It was Obama's first run, and there was a lot of speculation that the youth would win him this election. I put together a panel of college students and filmed myself asking them general questions about their involvement in the election. I had found that though youth were busy talking about the election, at least with the ones I interviewed, they weren't actually getting involved as much as the commentators had predicted. She had come to be a part of the panel, and I was grateful for her willingness to express her views on camera.

From what I remember, we talked about politics, boyfriends, ex-boyfriends, and school. She was attending Western Michigan University and was ranting about the lack of enthusiasm among youth for the election, one of the only issues we actually do see eye to eye on.

Posy-Rosy has an incredible sense of humor. She has this quick wit that really deserves its own daytime television slot. She is Jewish, not Adventist, and so her upbringing was very different than mine. She is much more apt to say what she is really thinking. Where I at times may have been fake, she is consistently real. She's not afraid to hurt your feelings, and if she thinks a joke is funny she tells it. She doesn't look around first to see who's listening.

At some point during our conversation the two women who were seated behind us got up and went to pay their bill. I was surprised, but then again not surprised, as one of the communications professors I had the pleasure of taking a class with during my undergraduate study stood up and revealed her existence. She tossed me a polite wave and smiled as she walked out of the door. Immediately I began running through my conversation up until that point in my mind. *Had I said anything incriminating? Was I too loud? Did I gossip? Did my friend here just say something inappropriate and now I am going to be guilty by association?*

"You gotta watch what you say around these parts, Thompson," Posy-Rosy said. "Every time we go somewhere it seems as though you run into someone you know. Do you still write in that Christian paper of theirs?" she asked.

She was agnostic at the time, though much has changed in her life since then. She moved a couple years ago, and after bringing balloons, a card, and an entire box of fruit leathers to her work (she loves fruit leathers), I gave her my real going-away present. This girl is like a sister to me. I have known her since I was 15 years old. I've watched her make bad decisions, and I've watched her make great ones. We've argued about our positions on God, and after so many years it seems some of my words rubbed off. I bought her a beautiful leather Bible and had her name inscribed on its cover. I also wrote a private message to her on the inside. I wasn't going to be around the corner anymore, and yet I wanted her to have sound advice at her fingertips. I am proud to say that today she is a Jew for Jesus.

I ignored her sarcastic comment about my little Christian paper. I was currently the Perspectives editor for the Andrews newspaper, but then again, she knew that.

"Yeah, I do," I answered.

"You really should get your act together then," she continued with a mouthful of lasagna and a condescending tone. "You never know who's watching."

As we finished our meal and made our way to the register, we found out that this one-horse town pizzeria did not take plastic. It was all cash or check. Cash to me is prehistoric, and I carry it . . . never. I asked the lady if we could run to the bank and make a withdrawal so we could come back and settle the tab. She said it was fine and was going to let us walk right out the door.

"Well, shouldn't I leave my ID or something?" I asked her, wanting to make sure she knew I had no plans on pulling a dine and ditch.

"OK. Sure," she answered. And with that we were off.

On the way back to the restaurant from the bank, I commented to my friend how only in a town as small as this would a restaurant owner not think twice about letting you walk out of the door on an unpaid bill without first collecting some collateral. I mean, had I wanted to, I could have left, walked out that door, never to be seen again.

As we were paying our bill, the owner indulged us in some casual conversation and mentioned to me some fact about myself that, to my surprise, indicated she knew of me. When I looked at her confused, she responded quickly, "Oh, I remember you because you were one of the queens, weren't you?"

In my younger years I had tried out for the town's beauty pageant. I didn't win. I did get first runner-up and some scholarship money for my first year of college, but that is a different story.

"Oh, yes, I was," I answered.

"Well, I guess it's a good thing we didn't stiff you," Posy-Rosy joked with her as we walked out the door. "You would have known how to find us."

I thought a lot about the encounter when I got home, and I wondered how many times people that knew me, and didn't feel the need to tell me they were there, had been watching me? I wondered how many people had caught me on a bad day, at a weak point, conforming to peer pressure, or being unfriendly, rude, cocky, or self-righteous? You see, I am guilty, at one time or another, of being all these things, and I guess I always assumed that if I wasn't recognized, it didn't happen. I've really been fooling myself, because even if people from my small town aren't there, Jesus Christ always is.

Shakespeare once said, "All the world's a stage," and the more I think about it, the more accurate this statement has become. Jesus, God, the Holy Spirit, angels, they're always there, and are always watching. I can appear flawless, and yet be riddled with blemishes. When God wants to take us home, what's going to matter will not so much be what everyone did see of me as much as what everyone didn't. It's who we are when we are with our closest friends, in a foreign state, or in the privacy of our rooms that will show where our heart is.

No matter whether you're from—a small town like mine or a big city where no one knows your name—I know Someone who knows exactly who you are. He has been watching you—good, bad, or indifferent—since day one. No, we never can be sure of exactly who may have been watching us. What we can be sure of is the one Man who always is.

"Before I formed you in the womb I knew you,
before you were born I set you apart."
—Jeremiah 1:5

Chapter 29

The Power of Prayer

Prayer is not asking. It is a longing of the soul.
It is a daily admission of one's weakness.
It is better in prayer to have a heart without words
than words without a heart.
—Mahatma Gandhi

A friend of mine called me once asking about prayer. She was not a "Christian" in the conventional sense of the word. She didn't go to church every weekend, or really any weekend at all. She didn't pay tithe, partake in Communion, get baptized, or read devotionals. She didn't do a lot of the things Christians need you to do in order to be "accepted" as one of them. However, she did pray.

It kind of annoys me when people discount someone else's personal experience with God because that person doesn't do it the way they do. Personal relationships are just that—personal. The key is not to separate someone by telling them they aren't in your "in crowd" until they do things the way you do. The first thing you should probably do is simply affirm them in their pursuit of any relationship at all. The best way to tell someone what the right doctrines are is simply to exemplify them.

Again, I think it is easy to be a Christian when your parents are Christians, your grandparents are Christians, and all your friends are Christians. Good for you. But that is simply not everyone's story. Some people actually have to choose God when it is not packaged and presented to them. I have a deep respect for that.

She called me because she wanted to have some girl talk about her boyfriend and, after some beating around the bush, mentioned she had been praying about their relationship. It was not unusual for my friends who weren't "Christians" to call and ask me questions about God. In fact, most of my friends who weren't "born again" did this because that was my role in our friendships. I was their "Christian friend," the go-to girl on spiritual endeavors. And when I was with my other friends from my private university who were raised in the church and did all the right things that my other set of friends didn't do, I referred to them as my "secular" friends. She bridged the gap this day, though, and I'll explain to you why.

She said she had been praying about her boyfriend, and then said she didn't know if she wanted to anymore. She is an independent person who likes to know what's going to be happening and is in complete control of her life. She said that she knew if she prayed to God about it that that meant it was going to be out of her control. She knew that once she said amen, she had asked God's will to supersede her own, and that scared her.

She called me that day to get advice from me. She wanted me to tell her that everything would be all right and perhaps quote from Scripture and let her know that God's will is always going to turn out better than your own. I gave that to her, and so we hung up. I don't think she realized, however, that it was actually *her* call that helped *me*.

Here she was, my "worldly" friend, my friend without the church and the private education, minus the "no drinking" and "no sex before marriage" regulations and lacking the Christian home upbringing along with the occasional *Chicken Soup* highlights. She was my "secular" friend, and yet she understood the power of prayer. She knew that praying meant dying to yourself. It meant asking God to take control of your situation because you couldn't deal with it anymore. Prayer was not just a routine ritual for her—it was a matter of life and death. It meant she'd have to step back and let God, a God I'd have thought she didn't even know, be God.

I then wondered how many of my "Christian" friends understood prayer the way she had that day. Was prayer a conscious effort to ask God to intervene, or was it casual? Had they become numb to Him? I can't give the answers to these questions. Only we can answer them for ourselves. I suppose we can tackle them then like a stack of dominoes, people changing themselves and then starting a revival. I can, however, look into my own life and tell you that it's been a little fifty-fifty. Sometimes I pray, and I don't even mean it. I ask for things I don't really think He'll ever give me, and I tell Him things I don't think He really hears. I, the one with every spiritually awakening tool at my disposal, forget the power of prayer 50 percent of the time, and that's pathetic.

One of the reasons I love reading the Bible is to see how these individuals, some who actually spoke to God and heard His reply, prayed. I am always awed by the reverence they used when approaching God. Abraham always said such things as "O Lord, If I have found favor in Your eyes at all, hear me on this," or Daniel when he says in Daniel 9:17, "'Now, our God, hear the prayers and petitions of your servant.'" My favorite prayer warrior is David. His prayers are chapters long and so beautiful and sincere. He says in 2 Samuel 7:18, "'Who am I, Sovereign Lord, and what is my family, that you have brought me this far?'" You see, these men understood prayer and knew who God was. They knew that not only was this their Father and Friend, but it was Christ, the Creator of the universe and Someone deserving of the utmost, intense respect.

What if we prayed as though we actually knew who God was and what He was capable of? What if we prayed like Christians, actual followers of Christ?

Sometimes I feel as if I understand a lot of things, and then God reminds me I still have much to learn. One thing I do know is this: My secular friend understands how prayer works, and now I'm wondering if I do.

This is the confidence we have in approaching God:
that if we ask anything according to his will, he hears us.
And if we know that he hears us—whatever we ask—
we know that we have what we asked of him.
—1 John 5:14, 15

Chapter 30

The Paradox

I have found the paradox, that if you love until it hurts,
there can be no more hurt, only more love.
—Mother Teresa

No matter who you are, where you're from, what you look like, or how you talk, there is one universal strike of the tongue that will send shivers down everyone's spine: "Yo mama."

Family is a pretty essential part of the average American's life. Everyone knows that a punch line about family could result with a punch in the face. You can insult the person, their clothes, their speech, perhaps even their dreams, but you better think twice before you slur someone's family, because usually that's when they'll snap.

One thing I've always known growing up is that I may have a million enemies, but they all seem quite small in comparison to my one sister. My sister has my back. She may not be emotional or shower me with hugs and kisses, but I've always known that if she saw me with tears in my eyes because of playground teasing, that bully was going to get a piece of my big sissy's mind.

She has done it time and time again. She has confronted big kids and small kids, girls or boys, it doesn't really matter, but it may change her approach. She obviously didn't come out swinging on some fifth-grade cohort of mine when she was in the much more prestigious eighth grade. But she would find whoever it was and simply say something like "What did you do to my sister?" and then ask them to explain why this was necessary. I'm not sure she ever encountered someone that decided to get lippy with her. She can be quite scary when she puts on her big-sister and protector face.

I've been thinking about the way it's ingrained in our society to stick up for those we love, and I wonder if we give the same gusto of loyalty to Christ. I've often thought highly of myself because I try to be open-minded. I've sat with atheists and heard their rants, bitter ex-Christians who have a score to settle, and misguided believers who are losing faith. I've been at a dinner table with people who have openly mocked my Lord, and I was silent. Sure, I may have interjected my arguments, said why I believed, and tried to give an objective counterpoint, but I sat still nonetheless. Had they mocked my earthly family I would have caused a scene and found the nearest exit, but since it was just my God, I guess it was OK. I traded loyalty to Christ for an "open mind" and an unbiased ear, and to be honest, I feel like a traitor.

Why is it that when it comes to our family or "our mamas" derogatory terms are fighting words, but when it is directed to the Giver of our breath we want to remain "politically correct"? The Bible stresses that Christ should be the object of our dearest affections, there should be no greater love than the love we build for Him, or else we have probably fallen short of what the Christian experience is actually about.

I've been reading the Bible through again, from the beginning, and I'm often starstruck by the power of God in the Old Testament. I think we forget that He is the same God today as yesterday. We forget that He poured His wrath on sinners, kept His people in bondage before He delivered Israel, and wiped out the entire earth with a flood. We forget that He is the same God and did not change. He is a backbone, not a wishbone—firm, not feeble. He forgives us when we crawl to Him, face in the dirt, snot in our nostrils, and tears in our eyes, and so we find Him soft.

We trick ourselves into thinking that we can get away with anything. He still demands obedience and respect. He could still destroy a city the way He extinguished Sodom and Gomorrah, and He could still cause a sea to drown an army of vengeful Egyptians. We replace His demands for reverence with friendship, and I think in doing so we lose a piece of the astonishment that should come with the fact that He allows a relationship at all. Even some of His closest biblical followers who spoke with Him and heard His voice still showed they were speaking to the King of the universe when they prayed.

Our biblical heroes such as Moses, David, Abraham, Isaac, and Joseph all often began their prayers with such words as "Lord, if I have found favor in Your eyes at all, hear me." You see, they knew who He was. They knew that even calling out His name meant inciting divine power, and so they approached Him accordingly. They knew the vast difference between the

Creator and the creation, and so they called out to Him in a humble manner.

And yet I can sit comfortably with people who mock Him and not even flinch. I watch movies that go against the very nature of what He stands for simply because "they're in." I think the human race, and especially my generation, has chipped away at His standards of moral living because we'd rather be "politically correct" than authentic. The big descriptor of intelligence today is "having an open mind." If you are certain of anything, well, then you are closed-minded.

How does this fit with our belief in Christ, though? How does certainty in the validity of the Bible, certainty in His return, certainty in the fact that He is Emmanuel, fit with my trying to be politically correct by being open-minded? When it comes to present truth, we have to be closed-minded. We have to be certain. We have to be confident in the fact that we know the answer.

I'm not saying that we shouldn't ever deal with people who believe differently than we do. I believe strongly that the church was called to go and be light in dark places, and I also believe that the closest to God someone else may get is you. I just think it's important to remember that when we go out and have these conversations, just who exactly it is we are speaking for. We shouldn't be sitting comfortably, because the end is near and the time is now. There is nothing comfortable about it.

I read this morning in Ellen White's book *Early Writings* about a vision God gave her in 1851 about the church of the last days. She says that many will not understand that in order to be standing when Christ returns you are going to need to be filled with the Spirit and reflect the image of Christ. "I also saw that many do not realize what they must be in order to live in the sight of the Lord without a high priest in the sanctuary through the time of trouble. Those who receive the seal of the living God and are protected in the time of trouble must reflect the image of Jesus fully" (p. 71).

Her last sentence on this page is "Let all remember that God is holy and that none but holy beings can ever dwell in His presence." After reading that this morning, I finally understand for the first time what it is going to take to be left standing as the last Christians in that last moment at Christ's return.

When Moses was in God's glory, the Israelites begged him not to come back down the mountain, for they feared being killed instantly by the sheer power in the residue of His holiness. Those who see God coming in the clouds will need to be able to stand, still human, as He returns. What patriarch has ever seen the face of God? What prophet, good teacher, or moral being has survived standing face to face with Jesus Christ? It is safe to assume that if it is your desire to live to see God return, you must start preparing your heart and soul now! I would guess that those who stand as the Son of Man appears from the heavens will need to be a reflection of Christ the way perhaps none have ever been before them. God will return. The question is whether or not you will begin preparing your character to meet Him.

So how do we prepare for this moment? We must prepare through the building of our personal relationship with Christ. We must prepare through devotionals, prayer, Scripture reading, silence, and intercessory work.

The pastor of my church once said something along these lines: "If the president of the United States asked you to be their ambassador, how many of us would not be elated? We would call all our friends and cause quite a commotion. We would have statuses on Facebook, hash tags on Twitter, photos and blogs telling anyone and everyone that we were selected for this important role of ambassador to this great country. Republican or Democrat, it wouldn't matter. The honor would have you reeling. We would be awestruck that the president of the United States of America knew who we were, knew our name, and chose us."

Why then do we think less of our mission from God to share His good news? I think first we have to get back to the basics. First, we have to remember who we are and who He is, because that relationship alone is a complete paradox. Your eyes are only still reading, your lungs are only still breathing, and your heart is only still beating, because He wills it to. He is Jesus, the one whom they called Christ. He is the Alpha and the Omega, the Beginning and the End. When the Bible says the earth was formless and void, it was He who fashioned something from nothing. This is not some casual friendship or a weekend at Bernie's. This is big stuff. He is the picture of holy, and the fact that that Guy wants anything to do with you and me is the definition of the word "paradox."

If you are wondering now about where you start in delivering this good news with others, let me share with you what I read in *Early Writings*. "There are many precious truths contained in the Word of God, but it is '*present truth*' that the flock needs now. I have seen the danger of the messengers running off from the important points of present truth, to dwell upon subjects that are not calculated to unite the flock and sanctify

the soul. Satan will here take every possible advantage to injure the cause"
(p. 63).

So what do we focus on? Present truth. We need to spend our efforts
uniting the flock and rallying the troops. What is present truth exactly? She
continues: "But such subjects as the sanctuary, in connection with the 2300
days, the commandments of God and faith of Jesus, are perfectly calculated
to explain the past Advent movement and show what our present position
is, establish the faith of the doubting, and give certainty to the glorious
future" (*ibid.*).

Ellen White says that present truth is God's imminent return, the Ten
Commandments, and messages of faith. Share your Sabbath in connection
with the Ten Commandments, share your knowledge of prophecy in
connection with His soon return, and share your testimony, as it will build
their faith. Share all of this present truth with a people who are thirsty for it.
But before you do that, recognize just exactly who you are an ambassador
for—Jehovah! And our Savior lives.

This is one of my absolute favorite Bible texts of all time, because it
shows just exactly who He is, how big He is, and how small we are:

Where were you when I laid the earth's foundation?
Tell me, if you understand. Who marked off its dimensions?
Surely you know! Who stretched a measuring line across it?
On what were its footings set, or who laid its cornerstone—while
the morning stars sang together and all the angels shouted for joy?
Who shut up the sea behind doors when it burst forth from the womb,
when I made the clouds its garment and wrapped it in thick darkness,
when I fixed limits for it and set its doors and bars in place, when
I said, "This far you may come and no farther; here is where your
proud waves halt"?
Have you ever given orders to the morning, or shown the dawn
its place, that it might take the earth by the edges and shake the wicked
out of it? The earth takes shape like clay under a seal; its features stand
out like those of a garment. The wicked are denied their light, and their
upraised arm is broken.
Have you journeyed to the springs of the sea or walked in the
recesses of the deep? Have the gates of death been shown to you? Have
you seen the gates of the deepest darkness? Have you comprehended the
vast expanses of the earth? Tell me, if you know all this.

What is the way to the abode of light? And where does darkness reside? Can you take them to their places? Do you know the paths to their dwellings? Surely you know, for you were already born! You have lived so many years!
Have you entered the storehouses of the snow or seen the storehouses of the hail, which I reserve for times of trouble, for days of war and battle? What is the way to the place where the lightning is dispersed, or the place where the east winds are scattered over the earth? Who cuts a channel for the torrents of rain, and a path for the thunderstorm, to water a land where no one lives, an uninhabited desert, to satisfy a desolate wasteland and make it sprout with grass? Does the rain have a father? Who fathers the drops of dew? From whose womb comes the ice? Who gives birth to the frost from the heavens when the waters become hard as stone, when the surface of the deep is frozen?
Can you bind the chains of the Pleiades? Can you loosen Orion's belt? Can you bring forth the constellations in their seasons or lead out the Bear with its cubs? Do you know the laws of the heavens? Can you set up God's dominion over the earth?
Can you raise your voice to the clouds and cover yourself with a flood of water? Do you send the lightning bolts on their way? Do they report to you, "Here we are"? Who gives the ibis wisdom or gives the rooster understanding? Who has the wisdom to count the clouds? Who can tip over the water jars of the heavens when the dust becomes hard and the clods of earth stick together?
Do you hunt the prey for the lioness and satisfy the hunger of the lions when they crouch in their dens or lie in wait in a thicket? Who provides food for the raven when its young cry out to God and wander about for lack of food?
—Job 38:4-41

Dating Made Practical

Lightning usually strikes only once in a lifetime . . .

Hook, Line, and Sinker
Heather Day Thompson

Heather Day Thompson invites you to walk a mile in her high heels so that you can avoid all the left turns that made her stumble. Using biblical concepts and stories from her own life, Heather tackles many of the challenges that you face, while emphasizing the importance of being anchored in the love of Christ. 978-0-8127-0504-1